DOUBLE MIRACLES IN DISCOVERY BAY, HONG KONG:

Personal Story Of Surviving Two Ruptured Brain Aneurysms

BOOK ONE

Marlegrecy N'Ovec, Ed.D.

XULON PRESS

Double Miracles In Discovery Bay, Hong Kong:
Personal Story Of Surviving Two Ruptured
Brain Aneurysms
by Marlegrecy N'Ovec, Ed.D.

Printed in the United States of America

ISBN 978-1-60647-249-1

www.xulonpress.com

In Memory

I honor the memory of Mabelle Maud Sloly my dear mother, who also survived a massive cerebral hemorrhage in 1986 without surgical intervention. She lived until May 16, 2005.

She left to me the legacies of strong, prayerful faith; unflinching courage to serve others; purity of purpose; spontaneous generosity and "emotional expansiveness."

She gave me plentiful opportunities to be patient and to constantly redefine my roles as a woman, a mother, an adult daughter, sibling, arbiter and care giver.

She taught me the true meaning of loving and forgiving unconditionally. She showed me how to solve problems without embarrassing anyone.

Her indomitable spirit and will to live have become mine. She lives on in my memory.

Dedication

Idedicate this book, with grateful appreciation, to my children Vidal Linton, Jessica Linton and Alaya Linton – Smith and their families. Others to whom I dedicate this book include my weekly prayer and Bible study partners of Discovery Bay; congregations of the Discovery Bay Anglican Church and the Discovery Bay International Community Church. I appreciate all who came to my rescue for both miracles. I thank those who visited me at home and in the hospital, including personnel from the American Embassy in Hong Kong, and those who prayed behind the scenes.

I greatly appreciate the service of the Discovery Bay Emergency Service that came to my rescue and got me swiftly to Princess Margaret Hospital.

I owe a huge debt of gratitude to surgeons, doctors, nurses, Pastoral and Intensive Care Personnel, Emergency, Neurological and Physiotherapy Departments of Princess Margaret Hospital. I will remember forever your saving my life through quick, decisive actions, surgery, medications, physical therapies, appropriate nutrition and unparallel daily care.

I thank all the children and their parents of the Pediatric Neurological Ward, who were my family for the greater part of thirty days, for their rejuvenating friendship.

I appreciate the sacrificial journey of Gracie GuoYan Ling of Dalian, China and Peggy Hui Yan of Dan Dong, China, and their families. Your coming to Hong Kong to care for me means more to me than I will be ever able to express. Xie xie nimen!

I wish everyone great health and abundant peace.

Acknowledgements

I acknowledge my Heavenly Father as the greatest orchestrator of my affairs, who makes the writing of this book possible. He, through His generous grace and mercy mobilized the persons, places and things that would play a vital role in both miracles and in the creation of this book.

Special Thanks

Many people played both direct and indirect roles in the creation of this book. I thank Ethan, Angela, Ada, Jane Sinclair of Hong Kong, Karen Chan, Florence Thomas and all who encouraged me to write. I am deeply grateful to:

Pastor Linus Lau for displaying confidence in my work by writing the foreword.

Transcribers

Members of the Youth Group of Chinese Baptist Church of Coral Springs, Florida

Samantha Cheng, Jessica Wong, Elizabeth Yuen, Jade Sun and Ammy Yuan

Takeisha Brown- Everett of The Life Christian Church, West Orange, N.J.

Proof Readers:

Lloyd G. Tapper, Jamaica, N.Y.; Mary- Alice Gage, Myrna Loy Currie, Ingrid Campbell, Jacqueline Bernard, Zhirong Gong, Steven Gong, Lynn –Chian Chen, Florence Zi-Qian Xion, Jae Zi-Zhen Xiong Calvin Chan –of Fort Lauderdale, Florida and E.W. Ubamaka, II- Hong Kong

Graphic Artists:

Cover Design: Tess Lia-Ching Leung – Chinese Baptist Church of Coral

Springs, Florida and David J. Smith - Life Christian Church, West Orange, New Jersey

Scenic Photographs for Cover: Lan May Cheong, Discovery Bay, H.K.

Cover Photograph of Marlegrecy and Mabelle

Brown's Photo Studio, Inc. Lauderhill Florida

Artists: Christingle - Ms. Anne Pinkman, Montclair, New Jersey **Shoes for your Journey -** Vidal R. Linton, Pompano Beach, Florida.

Computer / Technical Assistance

David J. Smith, Montclair, New Jersey; Jessica L Linton & Miles K. Discuillo, Pelham New York; Alaya and Micah Linton – Smith, Montclair, New Jersey; Everyl May Currie, Calgary, Alberta, Canada; Ted Donaldson, Ingrid Campbell *and Paul Miller- Paul's Tech Support, Fort Lauderdale Florida.*

Hospitality:

Lynn – Chian Chen, Gi -Ting Chen, Malvin Chen, Florence Zi-Qian Xiong, Jae Zi-Zhen Xiong, Ophelia Xu, Whinkle Leung, Jacky Leung, Anita Kwong, Susanna Li, Christine Li,

Adrienne Lam, Cassie Au, Susanna Li, Christine Li and other members of my Church family of Chinese Baptist Church Of Coral Springs

Special Assistance:

Novella Thomas and Elizabeth Anglin, Bronx, New York; Violet Nash, Fort Lee, N.J.; Jordan Linton-Smith, Montclair, N.J.; Floyd Dorsey, Gladys Aldana, Emlin Smith-Zayas and Ingrid Campbell, Ft. Lauderdale, Florida.

I thank everyone, who has assisted me in any way to make the completion of this book possible. I crave the forgiveness of anyone, whose name I might have uninten-

tionally omitted.

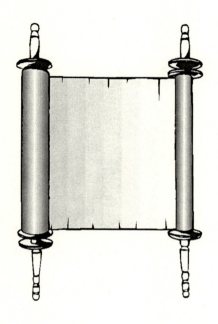

"Now go!

Write it before them in a table and write it in a book

That it may be for the time to come and forever"

Isaiah 30:8 KJV

Special Note

All names of persons in both miracles are ficti-
tious, except for my children or as otherwise stated.
Similarities to names of real persons are purely
coincidences.

Table of Contents

Foreword

As she promises in her introduction, Marlegrecy takes us down her memory lane on a journey that is enriched by her personal encounter with our living God. Through her near-death experience and survival from ruptured brain aneurysms, she introduces us to a God, who is good, faithful, and almighty. Her story offers hope for all who are going through "the valley of the shadow of death."

It is a personal account of someone whose faith has been severely tested and how she persevered and held onto God's sure and precious promises.

As you walk with her, you will feel as if you were right there gazing into the countenance of death. You will experience how she struggled to cope with her physical impairment and how she triumphed against all odds.

It causes one to break forth in jubilant singing:

Where, O death is your sting?

Where, O death is your victory? (I Corinthians 15:55)

Marlegrecy's story is a reminder, once again, of the victory that Christ has won for us through His painful death and glorious resurrection and of the hope we have as we look forward to the consummation of such a victory upon His second coming.

I am also deeply moved by her dedication to serving others. She has been serving the Chinese people in Jamaica, Mainland China, Hong Kong and the United States since 1995 in various capacities as an international family and community educator despite the language and cultural challenges.

Following the footsteps of many pioneers she, by faith, ventured into unfamiliar territories and simply trusted God to supply her needs. She put herself at risk to edify others by teaching English and other subjects in various educational settings in Mainland China, Thailand and Hong Kong.

"How beautiful are the feet of those who bring good news!" (Romans 10:15)

is an appropriate reference for Marlegrecy.

It was during her tenure in Hong Kong, in 2002 she experienced the power of double Miracles, when her merciful Father saved her twice from death by ruptured brain aneurysms.

<u>Double Miracles in Discovery Bay, Hong Kong...</u> is for everyone. This story of her surviving ruptured brain aneurysms will inspire you to tell of your miracles from God. Enjoy and be blessed!

Linus S. Lau, Senior Pastor
Chinese Baptist Church,
Coral Springs, Florida

Introduction

A single miracle is a remarkable event, but double miracles in any place, and in Discovery Bay, Hong Kong in particular, are marvelous events and incredible happenings.

What is a miracle? According to most dictionaries, *"A miracle is a marvel, a wonder, an abnormal or extraordinary event manifesting divine intervention in human affairs. It is a wonderful example or action that apparently contradicts or defies conventional wisdom and scientific laws and is thought to be supernatural"*
(DK Pockets English Dictionary, page 267, 2003)

This definition fits perfectly in the fabric of this story.

Now, think of someone having two detrimental, life-threatening events in the same geographical location sixty-nine days apart and surviving both. I believe many would say these were miracles, and they are stories worth hearing. I agree, so I wrote my story of surviving two ruptured brain aneurysms and one brain surgery.

This book is a first-hand account of such happenings. Between September 19, 2002, and November 24, 2002, I was the blessed receiver of double miracles in Discovery Bay, Hong Kong. In retrospect, these two spectacular places with an ingrained flavor of the miraculous seemed to have been the "chosen" settings for my miracles. I believe my survival was largely due to my living in Discovery Bay on Lan Tau Island, Hong Kong among people who cared. To borrow a cliché, it was not just, "Being in the right place at the right time". It was more than that. It was being in a preordained miracle site and among people, who were pre-appointed to be active participants in two miracles

In the first miracle on September 19, 2002, two Australian ladies, with whom I was praying, rescued me when I blacked out and lost awareness. They cared for me. They protected me from potential, self- inflicted harm. Later, they invited a group of men and women, mutual friends and acquaintances, to my apartment to witness my dilemma and to pray. Their fervent prayers saved me from death.

This is second hand knowledge, told to me, since I was totally unaware of all the happenings and of all the people with whom I interacted after I fainted in a prayer gathering in The Greens in Discovery Bay, Hong Kong. The fact that I survived the first ruptured brain aneurysm without medical intervention, attests to the superior care my rescuers gave me and to the power of their prayers.

In the second miracle on November 24, 2002, my Canadian friend, who lived close by me in Peninsula Village of Discovery Bay on Lan Tau Island, left her house guests to accompany me in an ambulance, along with the Discovery Bay Emergency crew, to the Princess Margaret Hospital to try and solve the mystery of the worst headache of my life.

This time, while at home, I was fully aware of everything except the reason for the headache. Could it have been just a serious migraine? I felt differently. I recalled the experience of a friend in Fort Lauderdale, who had been having chronic migraine headaches for several years. For her, the pain is intense and often crippling. Although I had similar symptoms, like persistent pain and sensitivity to light, the stiffness in my neck and throbbing in the right side of my head added an element of urgency. It was not just a migraine headache. I did not know what it was, but I felt I needed help, "yesterday". It felt that urgent.

When my headaches intensified and became resistant to all home remedies and conventional interventions, I called 999, the emergency number for Hong Kong to get much needed help. I had learned this number just a week before my headaches started. The efficiency of the Discovery Bay Emergency Service and the professional actions of the two courteous, empathetic paramedics played a vital part in getting me swiftly to the Princess Margaret Hospital.

My story is an outpouring of gratitude. I consider myself the most thankful woman alive. I am most grateful for all the interventions, which saved me from death twice. I deeply appreciate and cherish the love, care, prayers and practical help of all who came to my rescue when I was totally unaware of the dangers I faced.

I am equally and deeply grateful to my Australian, American, Canadian, Chinese, Filipinos, British and Scottish friends, pastors and their families, who supported me throughout my ordeals in the Greens and Peninsula Village of Discovery Bay, Hong Kong; during and after my brain surgery at Princess Margaret Hospital and my recovery in my home.

An Invitation

I invite you to journey with me down a memory lane designed to recapture memories of the miracles of our lives and of people we know. As you interact with me by reading this story, it is my hope it will inspire you to tell your stories of events, which superseded human control and conventional wisdom, even if you do not believe in miracles.

My double miracles happened in Discovery Bay, Hong Kong, approximately twelve thousand miles from the Discovery Bay and the Princess Margaret Hospital of my native Jamaica in the Caribbean. Wherever your huge miracles happened, give them a voice, so others may hear of the power of our mutual creator, who says, *"Write in a book all the words, I have spoken to you". Jeremiah 30: 2 NIV.*

Setting The Stage

Chapters one through four are stage setters. They tell how I got to China and Hong Kong. Chapters five through eleven paint a portrait of the timely developments, some of which are mini miracles, leading up to the major events. I believe there are no coincidences, no mistakes, no should haves, could haves, would haves in my double miracles. Everyone, every place, everything, every event, *was carefully pre- ordained and orchestrated. They took place as they were meant to happen.*

In no way do I discount the feelings and evaluative comments of anyone who has a different opinion. In a sense, I "was not there" when the first miracle happened, as you will see in **"Dead Woman Walked".**

I trust you will enjoy reading <u>Double Miracles in Discovery Bay, Hong Kong</u>…. May it encourage you to be vigilant about your own health and the health of your family. May it also inspire you to tell, write and publish the stories of your divinely preordained miracles.

I thank you for listening. I wish you exquisite health.

Marlegrecy N'Ovec, Ed.D

Fort Lauderdale, Florida

Montclair, New Jersey

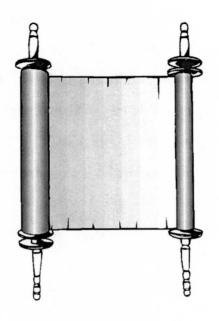

"...Leave your country, your people and your father's household and go to the land I will show you"

Genesis 12:1 (NIV)

1

Why Hong Kong And China?

"Childhood Fascination"

My story of surviving two ruptured brain aneurysms in Discovery Bay, Hong Kong happened in the year 2002, but the journey to Hong Kong began long before I left my native Jamaica. Hong Kong and China had always fascinated me from my Calabar Elementary school years in Kingston. I thought my longing to know where in the world these countries are located would one day become a reality. I wanted to see them for myself instead of just locating them on a map in my geography class.

Since 1961, Jamaica's motto has been, "Out of many one people". Chinese has been one of the many racial groups in Jamaica for much longer. Some historians dated Chinese presence in the "New World" before Columbus visited, and others dated them to the seventeenth century when slavery flourished in the Caribbean. Their journey to Jamaica is the topic of a future publication.

Throughout all my days in Jamaica, from infancy to adulthood, I socialized with Chinese. In my early childhood in Mandeville, my birthplace, Chinese owned, and still own, many of the large wholesale and retail businesses. I still remember the large "Emporium" which seemed to carry everything "under the sun". They sold the largest variety of merchandise from groceries to household goods. Chinese also owned most of the fabric stores in Mandeville.

When my mother and I moved from Mandeville, we relocated in Central Kingston, which was similar to a modern "China Town". We lived among Chinese, who came mainly from Hong Kong and Mainland China. In my young mind, there was no difference between the two countries.

Chinese children were my classmates and playmates. Their parents were the community's grocers, bakers, merchants, dry cleaners, numbers organizers and a host of other service providers. There were Chinese businesses on almost every corner in my neighborhood.

My family shopped often at the one at Smith Lane and Sutton Street. I still remember the name of the family, who owned the grocery store. I will call them "Lai". I recall the beautiful faces of the children, who were offspring of mixed marriages between Chinese and Jamaicans of African descent.

I enjoyed going to Lai's grocery. One of the thrills was to pick up small pieces of salted cod fish that chipped off when they chopped up a whole dried cod into smaller pieces. The neighborhood children, including me, liked to pick up pieces of fish from around the chopping block.

SURPRISE!!!!!!!

One day, I picked up a pretty piece, which looked liked a piece of delicious codfish. I could not wait to sink my teeth in it! AHHHHHHHHHHHHHHHH!!!!!! When I did, it turned out to be a piece of brown soap. YUK!!!!!!!! I spat and spat to get the soapy taste out of my mouth. I had to rush home to wash my mouth with cool water. We were not sure if it were a deliberate plan to stop us from picking up the fish scraps, but it certainly stopped me.

Chinese businesses dotted Wildman Street, where I lived, from one end to the other. During my late elementary school days, the bakery at Wildman and Beaston Streets was where I bought hot, delicious sourdough (hard dough) bread bursting with butter or stuffed with pieces of fatty pork. Many days, a piece of this yummy bread, pieces of rejected banana and a mug of milk or lemonade was lunch for my brother and me.

When I attended Kingston Technical High School on Hanover Street, another Chinese grocery with the items high – school students fancied, was our favorite rendezvous. We ate lunch, listened to our favorite songs on the radio and just hung out there. The shop was on the lane adjacent to the school, so we could hear the first warning bell before the lunch period ended. We would sometimes wait for the bell to ring then ran fast to get on campus before the final bell rang. Being late was not an option for us.

One of my deepest childhood interests was in the Chinese Language. Quite often, after taking my brother to his day care at the YMCA at North Street, I liked to walk over to the Chinese School at East Street to listen to the young Chinese boys and girls learn to speak their language. The memory is still fresh. I remember the face of the teacher. She was a darker complex-ioned Chinese although her facial features were just as aqui-line as any fair skinned Chinese. She wore her hair pulled back from her beautiful face to a large, perfectly formed bun at the nape of her elegant neck. She had colorful chopsticks on both sides of her bun. She wore beautiful clothes, but I was not sure if they were traditional Chinese attire.

Her students were all Chinese and predominately boys. They wore khaki shorts and shirts. The girls wore a dark skirt with white blouse. I used to look at them from outside an opened classroom window. I listened without understanding what she was teaching them, but I felt she was my teacher, too. I quietly or silently mimicked what she was saying.

When I picked up my brother Ricardo, seven years my junior, I would try out my "Chinese" on him. He thought I could really speak well although he did not understand a word of it. When I got home and pretended to be speaking Chinese, the people in my home, who heard me, thought I was crazy. They told me to "scram" and reminded me I was "NOT Chinese". I was just having fun day-dreaming about something I knew I would learn some day. I had the ambition as well as the desire to study Chinese.

When I attended undergraduate teachers' college in Jamaica, Chinese students were once again my "batch mates" or my seniors. One of the seniors, a brilliant Chinese woman, excelled in both academics and extracurricular activities and was voted the best dancer of the Cha-cha-cha. Then and now, Chinese in Jamaica are notable musicians, painters, sculptors, acrobats and other performing artists. They are also professionals in every discipline and field of work including engineering, law and medicine. Chinese permeate every aspect of Jamaican life and culture.

Celebrating Chinese New Year in my childhood was one of the most exciting events for me. It was replete with tons of fireworks and lasted at least one week. The food was most appetizing. I stuck to eating the fruits, vegetables and noodles. I cultivated a taste for fresh, sweet lychee and preserved, tart Chinese plums. Chinese apples ranked highly on my list of favorite fruits. I still enjoy a juicy pomegranate.

Closer Home

I interacted with Chinese not only in my community, elementary and high schools, college, church and other places, but also in my family. There are Chinese, still living, on the side of my maternal grandmother in my family. One of our most beloved cousins, Salome is "half Chinese". Her several occupations include being an accomplished seam-stress. She was sought out by many. Future brides, bridal parties and others, who wanted exquisitely tailored clothes, hired her. She made me some of my most beautiful clothes.

Well - founded Reason

Having Chinese ancestry made me more curious and determined to find out more about Chinese customs, language and country. I was intrigued by the way the Chinese in Jamaica lived where they worked. All the families, who owned businesses, especially grocery shops and laundries, lived either in an apartment above or in the back of the business. I used to think this was such a "neat" idea. Their wisdom of combining workplace and residence saved money time and energy. It also provided, most of the time, an element of security for the employees and residents, who were, more likely than not, members of the same family.

Abiding curiosity or Insane Plan?

This Chinese life style piqued my curiosity. I wanted to find out if life in the homeland was similar to life in Jamaica. The stories confirming some of what I saw in Jamaica were not enough. I wanted first hand proof. The best way to find out, I thought, was to visit their countries of origin. The same folks, who said I was "crazy" to pretend I could speak Chinese as a child, also thought I was totally insane to want to travel to China and Hong Kong.

A Pledge to Keep

I pledged I would see these two nations, which gripped my heart and powered aspects of my imagination, even if I had to wait for two life times. I listened repeatedly to the song, "I want to take you on a slow boat to China.". It kept my longing alive, but it also made me think. I thought long and hard about the distance between Jamaica and China and Hong Kong. Since they are over ten thousand miles away, going there on "a slow boat" would take forever! I might not even get there. I dreaded this thought.

I tried to create mental pictures of how the country might look. I imagined things about the people, their homes, the weather, their clothes, their money and their children. After learning about the dynasties and about Confucius and how his teachings influenced Chinese education system, I was determined to keep my pledge to seek opportunities to travel to Hong Kong and China.

OPPORTUNITIES KNOCK?

Although my travels took me first to the United States of America, I never lost my hope of seeing these two Asian countries. While I was studying in New York at Columbia University in 1991, I responded to an advertisement for teachers to work in Hong Kong as English instructors. I felt comfortable applying for the position of English instructor although teaching English was not my discipline then. I had a Jamaican based British, early education. I was qualified in Language Arts, Special Education and English as a Second Language (ESL) and currently specializing in Family and Community Education at the doctorial level.

The salary offers were attractive, but what lured me was the chance of finally fulfilling my childhood dreams of traveling to Asia. I wanted to have the opportunity to study Chinese culture and language. If getting to Hong Kong through a teaching position were the way then I would go for it. I applied for the teaching position. I got no response.

I wondered why the prospective employer did not even acknowledge getting my application. After reading an article about the high premium employers in Hong Kong place on resumes, I felt confident mine would make the mark. I had spent much time developing an objective, professional resume. What else should I do? I decided to WAIT.

I recalled some of Keller's words about how no opportunity is ever lost. They are gathered up and some time in the future, when we are truly ready for them, we get them back. I *pondered these thoughts in my heart. I believed at the appointed time I would get to Hong Kong.*

I will have something worthwhile in the forms of talents and knowledge to take on my journey. Best of all, I will not have to travel on a "slow boat." A "fast jumbo jet" will take me there in less than twenty-four hours. I waited patiently for that day to arrive.

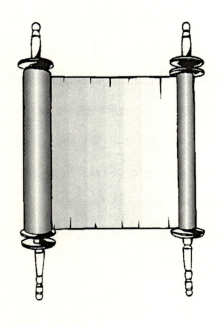

"I ran these marathons early

on Saturday mornings

between 4:00 a.m. and 7:00 a.m.,

so I missed the bulk of strolling vacationers,

the cruising automobiles and most importantly

the heat of the scorching Florida sun"

2

China First?

Cross Roads

In 1993, while working as an assistant professor of English and Developmental Studies in a university in South Florida, I responded to another invitation to teach in Hong Kong. Again, I applied. Again, I got no response. I placed the idea of teaching in Hong Kong on a "sabbatical" back burner while I worked toward tenure in my current position of assistant professor and Chair of the English Department.

Another Invitation

In early 1995, I received an attractive brochure with an invitation to teach English in China. These brochures had been coming in the mail for about seven years even when I was seeking a teaching position in Hong Kong. I was the one not responding this time. The tables were turned.

After I read the brochure, and viewed an accompanying video "…Cross Roads" on China's Higher Education system, they led me to consider teaching English in China. The invitation was to teach English in various cities in China for a summer, a year or two years. I read the slim brochure repeatedly.

What an Idea!

There was nothing in it about Hong Kong, nor was there any information about attractive salary packages. Instead, people who wanted to teach in China under the "umbrella" of the California-based sending organizations had to pay them an administrative fee by raising their own support. It is prudent to withhold the name of the organizations since I have no permission to identify them.

At first I thought this was insane. I wanted to earn huge sums of money to pay off my student loans, care for my children and live well. Then I recalled dedicating my degrees, expertise and talents to "Kingdom Economy." I had prayed for directions and opportunities to serve where I would be called.

This dedication, my childhood interaction with the Chinese in Jamaica and my longing to know Hong Kong and China, made my decision relatively easy; however, I felt I, too, was at a cross roads. I accepted the challenge to teach Chinese students, in China, English for summer 1995.

Paving the Road to China

The Marathons

I raised funds for my field service through several, personal – one -woman – marathons. Family, friends, and church members and strangers each endorsed a certain number of miles for a certain amount of money. Some folks just gave a generous donation without exacting that I run miles. Wonderful!

I walked or ran several ten, fifteen and twenty miles marathons, over a period of two months. My most frequent round-trip route originated from and ended at my home in East Gates, Lauderdale Lakes. This route took me to the beautiful Fort Lauderdale Beaches, which are the popular destinations of many spring breakers and home of the famous, annual "Air and Sea Show."

"Marathoning" along Sunrise Boulevard and the picturesque Highway A1A was exciting! Here are many beaches with lazing beachcombers, loud crashing waves, and squawking seagulls. Showy man – of – war fancied flying overhead and swooping down when it suited them. The street is usually crowded with strolling vacationers and cruising automobiles. The sights are breathtaking. To complete my marathons, I returned via the two of Fort Lauderdale's traffic filled streets: Oakland Park Boulevard and State Road Seven.

I ran these marathons early on Saturday mornings between 4:00 a.m. and 7:00 a.m., so I missed the bulk of strolling vacationers, the cruising automobiles and most importantly the heat of the scorching Florida sun. I liked the sounds of the loud crashing waves, the squawking seagulls and showy man – of – war.

Balancing Act Plus

Sometimes, for improving my posture, I walked the entire ten or fifteen miles with a basket of fruits or gallon water bottle on my head. I often ended up getting more than improved posture. I got unwanted attention from male passersby. I often responded with, "No thank you; God bless you; have a good day." I was never afraid or deterred. I had a goal to fulfill.

After raising substantial funds, I joined a group of eighty-eight other teachers, who were also headed for China, in California for two weeks of orientation. We were trained in methods of teaching English as a Second Language (ESL), Chinese culture, and in survival Chinese before leaving for Mainland China.

The entire group stayed in Beijing for another week of training and learning about Chinese culture. From Beijing we were "deployed" to various sites in different cities to demonstrate the art of English Communication mainly to enthusiastic Chinese teachers. My team of thirteen was sent to a teachers' college on a hill in a modern, elevated seaport city.

This place reminded me of Mandeville, the southern city in Jamaica, where I was born. Mandeville and the assigned Chinese City have mountains, lush vegetation, beautiful floral landscaping and salubrious climate. These make them inviting and captivating for many people.

The experience was exhilarating!

After completing fieldwork in the assigned cities, we returned to Beijing where all eighty-nine teachers reconvened for debriefing and departure to the many states in America from which we came. We shared the highs and low points of our experience and evaluated its effect on the Chinese teachers with whom we had interacted. The positives far-out weighed the "imported" negatives I encountered. It was for me an exhilarating and energizing experience.

What About Hong Kong?

Hong Kong was still on my "sabbatical back burner" I had made no connections between the two nations. It was not until the end of summer '95 Hong Kong came back to my mind. In August 1995 when we were leaving Beijing, and groups of women, including First Lady Hillary Clinton, were arriving for an international conference on human rights for women, the subject of Hong Kong resurfaced.

Several soothsayers were predicting a "bloody take-over" of Hong Kong from the British by China in August 1997. Westerners were warned to stay out of Mainland China and Hong Kong during the take-over. It was doubtful the California- based organization would be sending teachers to anywhere in Asia in 1997.

It meant little to me since I had no near-future intent to return to China, and I entertained no imminent hope of seeing Hong Kong. So I thought. Hong Kong was still simmering on my mental "back-burner" with no aroma or steam rising to remind me of my desire to go there.

My summer '95 experience left an incredibly sweet taste in my mouth as far as my initial contact with the Mainland Chinese was concerned; I wanted to return there when another opportunity came my way.

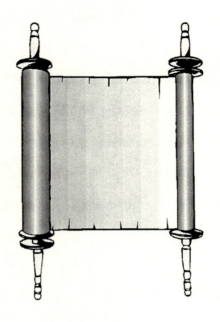

"The young woman, Mary,

who had become my first Chinese "daughter"

in 1995, referred me to the dean of her alma

mater."

3

Three Years Later

Back To China

When my contract at the university in South Florida ended on a "bitter – sweet" note in 1998, it were as if I had received a huge gift of time to spend however I wished. I headed back to China. This time it was for a whole year.

The young woman, Mary, who had become my first Chinese "daughter" in 1995, referred me to the dean of her alma mater. She said she would have felt honored if I were to accept a position to lecture there in English and Theory of Education.

I felt she honored me. She had known me for only three years, yet she confidently referred me to the dean and the human resources department of the university from which she graduated with a bachelor degree. She, herself, was an English educator in another university.

I accepted the position although I was previously offered one in another city and university through the new sponsoring organization.

It was also based in California as the one that sponsored me in 1995. They worked with me and willingly switched me with someone who needed a position elsewhere in China.

The experience as an educator in English and education courses broadened my horizons and taught me much about Chinese culture. It was a pleasure- filled experience. I enjoyed relationships, which were pleasantly new to me with both faculty and students and with people from outside the academic community.

I liked my life immensely during this year. At its end, I felt I had achieved several milestones and satisfied my childhood desire to live in China.

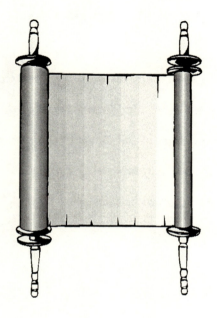

"She had been most caring,

affectionate and attentive.

Because of her, my first year in China

was productive and life – changing".

A Tribute to A Daughter

Mary, my first Chinese "daughter" and I met on my first trip to China in 1995. She was part of the crowds who gathered on weekends at the "English Corners" in the town square to hear native speakers of English. At one of these gatherings, she approached me and said, "You again!" I found her exclamation amusing. We chuckled. I liked her instantly.

She remained with the crowd and asked questions about America's healthcare system and the general care of its senior citizens. She told me of China's attitude to its elderly and dramatic sociological changes in the structure of the family.

Later, she told me she was an English educator at an university and was interested in improving her English as well as learning more about different cultures. She said she wanted her students to become truly knowledgeable of the new world to which China was opening up. She often brought her students to "culture night" at the teachers' college where I volunteered. She had many questions to ask and much information to give.

During my six weeks stay in her city, she took a personal interest in the group of educators and in me. She offered her help to make our stay enjoyable and fruitful. Several times within a week, she would visit the hotel where we were staying to make sure we were well and had all we needed.

After I returned to America in 1995, we wrote to each other frequently and telephoned occasionally. We developed a close friendship. She started calling me her "American mother". She said she meant no disrespect of her own mother to whom I was close in age; however, she felt close enough to me, despite our nationality and racial differences, to think of me as a mother.

She told me about important aspects of her life and work and sought my advice for problems just like my own daughters did. Our admiration for each other grew steadily until it felt like a true mother – daughter relationship. I called her "daughter" and told her about my family. I told my two daughters and son of her. They welcomed the idea of having a Chinese "sibling" and periodically asked about her and their "nephew".

In 1998, she invited me to work at her alma mater. I accepted a position to teach English and Theory Of Education. The result was a year of interesting experiences for both of us and personal growth for me.

She inducted me into her family. Her brilliant son Andrew became my first Chinese "grandson" and her husband Dennis became my first Chinese "son-in-law".

I met her mother, brother and other relatives, and enjoyed their gracious hospitality. Mary was one of the most thoughtful and generous persons I had the privilege of meeting in China.

Mary died in 2006. Her untimely death saddened me as if she were my own daughter. She was still quite young in her early forties, I believe. She had been most caring, affectionate and attentive. Because of her, my first year in China was productive and life - changing. She directly and indirectly taught me lessons about traditional Chinese culture, customs and history that I would not have learned otherwise.

This is a small tribute to Mary and her family, but I will seek an opportunity to honor her memory and her family in a more meaningful way soon.

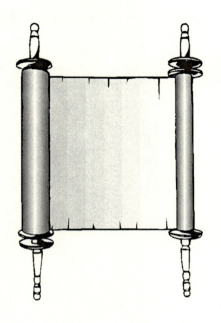

"Blessed be the Lord for He has shown me

His marvelous kindness in a *strong city*"

Psalm 31:21

4

Hong Kong At Last

"A Strong City"

While lecturing at my "daughter's" alma mater in China, I met Gabi, an American woman, who lived with her husband, their two sons and a household helper in Hong Kong. Our meeting was stamped "miraculous." I reserve the details for another book. An excerpt will suffice here. I met this stranger in the hotel lobby of the university campus hotel where she was staying for a weekend and where I was living for a year.

I had been studying for hours in my room and decided to take a break. I arrived in the lobby the same time as Gabi. We exchanged pleasantries, and we discovered we had mutual friends among the American students, who were studying Chinese in the university where I worked. Suddenly, I felt Gabi and I were old friends. I invited her to my hotel suite. She accepted. We spoke for several minutes about our family backgrounds and our reasons for being in our respective countries.

Before our brief visit ended, Gabi was crying. I thought I had offended her, but she said her tears were joyful. I did not know whether to feel honored or embarrassed. She assured me again all was well, and she was just glad to have met me.

She was impressed by the way we both came to the lobby at the same time to take a break. She said it confirmed we were meant to meet. At the time, I thought it was just a plain, old coincidence and nothing else. We exchanged contact information. Hers was extensive. Gabi included several ways to get in touch with her, her husband and even her housekeeper. She gave me an open invitation to visit her family in Hong Kong.

I thanked her for her generosity, but I thought, "Not a sweet chance"!

A few days after meeting Gabi, my administrators called to say they would be arranging for the team of teachers and supporting staff to spend part of the three weeks mid year break for rest and recreation (R&R) in Hong Kong. I thought I was imagining things. I recalled my new friend – Gabi's tears and her invitation. Was this a mere coincidence? Now, it seems I do have a "sweet chance" to visit Hong Kong. I informed my administrators I would like to go ahead of the team to visit with a friend and then connect with the team of teachers later.

They agreed with my plan. I called Gabi and told her the good news then made my airline reservation. The administrators would make the necessary travel arrangements for the rest of the group and for my return to China and tell me the itinerary. I became excited about finally having an opportunity to visit Hong Kong.

When they called, it was not with an itinerary for a Hong Kong vacation. The venue was changed to Thailand because of some problems with the Hong Kong site and high airline fares. I thought my dream to visit Hong Kong was shattered. I called Gabi and told her of the changes. She sensed my disappointment. She assured me there would be other opportunities and encouraged me to, "Cheer up". I was able to camouflage my disappointment with cheery smiles. My full teaching schedules kept my mind off Hong Kong. This lasted for a few days.

The administrators called again to say in order to get the lowest airfare to Thailand, I had to take an evening flight and stop overnight in Hong Kong on both legs of the flight. Unbelievable! I had a chance to be in Hong Kong, for at least two nights. I called Gabi again and told her of the changes.

"What did I tell you? Now, see you have another opportunity. There are NO coincidences!"

I apologized for the confusion. Her response was, "No apologies, please. It is all part of the plan". She sounded confident. I was contemplative.

Gabi and her family invited me to stay with them overnight on my way to and from Thailand. On the return portion of my trip, they extended the overnight to two weeks. I had time to see some of the highlights and tourist attractions in Hong Kong such as Victoria Peak, the flower markets, museums and the Star Ferries. I met many wonderful people and had different satisfying experiences.

I could smell some aroma coming from the "back-burners." Hong Kong was steaming again in my consciousness. I had a decision to make. I asked myself, "Should I remain in China for another year, or should I move to Hong Kong?"

Three Gifts

Gabi and her family, who introduced me to this "miraculous" place, gave me three things: an opened ended invitation to return; encouragement and a warning. They said their doors were open to me. They gave me important contacts for future employment, but she warned that at my advanced age, the "organized chaos" that was endemic to Hong Kong, may overwhelm me. I considered their advice gifts, and I used them as part of the framework for making my decision to migrate to Hong Kong.

Following My Heart

After returning to China, I thought deeply about our discussion and prayed earnestly for direction for my course of action at the end of the one-year contract in China. I awaited some kind of strong indications for my next move. When the director of my sending organization asked,

"How would you like to go to Hong Kong to teach English?"

My thought was, "Are you kidding me? Do I ever!"

My quick response was a definite "Yes"!

Later, I discovered the recruiting organization required couples to serve together for the duration of the contract. My husband must accompany me. This is a commitment he would not make for various reasons. Three months would be the maximum time he wanted to spend away from Florida. He encouraged me to sign the contract, and he would have joined me for three months. We thought it over carefully, counted the cost on several levels and decided to decline the offer.

A Gem

This situation motivated me to become an independent education consultant. I decided to evaluate all the instructions; tips and encouragement I got then use the excellent bits and follow my heart go to Hong Kong. I had my husband's encouragement and blessings. Moving to Hong Kong, which was once called, "Jewel of the Imperial Crown," was a gem of a decision for me to have made in 1999. Hong Kong became a "strong city" for me in many ways.

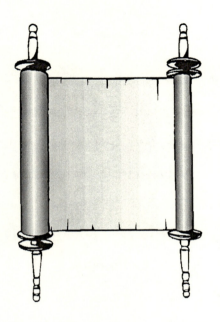

"The stranger, who welcomed me at Hong

Kong's

humungous airport,

was "Nancy", a young, dynamic, Chinese

woman.

She was a close friend of "Paula", an impressive,

Chinese, entrepreneur, whom I had met

in a cultural center in China in 1998".

5

Like Father Like Daughter

Going to Hong Kong this time had an Abrahamic flavor. My decision resembled the biblical patriarch, Abram's response to the command:

"Get you out of your country and from your kindred and from your father's house unto a land which I will show you... and I will bless you..."
(Genesis 12:1-2)

Abram's response was unquestioning and spontaneous: **"So, Abram departed as the Lord had spoken...."**
(Genesis 12:4)

This was before his name was changed to Abraham. I also had a name change, which I will write about in the sequel to this story.

I believed I, too, was following a command to venture into the unknown. I did not know where in Hong Kong and to whom I was going. Believing all would be well, despite the earlier warnings, I went. On the way to Hong Kong, I met Cleo and her infant son Jae on the airplane. I watched Jae whenever Cleo needed a break. Later, they and their family become an important part of my journey to the unknown. This story will fill another volume.

The stranger, who welcomed me at Hong Kong's humungous airport, was Nancy, a young, dynamic, Chinese woman. She was a close friend of Paula, an impressive, Chinese, entrepreneur, whom I had met in a cultural center in China in 1998. Together, they were my "hospitality committee". They worked out the logistics of meeting me in Hong Kong and of providing living accommodation.

Nancy sheltered me in her larger apartment, to which she had moved a few days before my arrival in August 1999.

When Paula had called her from China to ask her the favor of receiving me, she said she was glad she had just moved to a larger place, and she would be happy to welcome me to a room of my own. Was this a coincidence?

This, to me, was the fruit of faith and the graciousness of Chinese hospitality since Nancy and I had never met. Nancy accommodated me for three weeks. She led me methodically through the "organized chaos" of which Gabi and her family had spoken. Speedily, Nancy helped me with revising my resume. She walked me through the classified sections of The South China Morning Post and other employment publications. She taught me the art of traveling by buses and trains in Hong Kong's extensive, efficient, public transportation system. I quickly learned the essentials for surviving unscathed by the pressures of daily living in super busy Hong Kong. I felt truly blessed.

Additionally, Nancy escorted me to a church service and introduced me to someone in Human Resources in a private school. The meeting resulted in an offer of a teaching position to me. By November 1999, two months after my arrival,

I was legally employed to teach first graders English as a Second Language (ESL). A dream had become reality.

Nancy was like a protective mother hen. She sacrificed her personal space to ensure my safety and enjoyment. I learned new lessons in survival and self - preservation. I realized how little can become much and how necessity is indeed "the mother of invention."

Living Well on Little

Nancy provided me with sleeping accommodation and meals for one week. Thereafter, she would continue to provide housing, but I would have to provide my own meals.

"No problems mon"! (Jamaicanese)

Since I had come to Hong Kong with only twenty American dollars, I had to be more than frugal. I had to be almost miserly. I had to invent ways to stretch the twenty dollars as far as it could reach for as many days as I would have to await more funds.

I allowed one large navel orange and a banana to serve me for three meals. I drank much boiled water instead of tea. I purchased small amounts of discounted products and made them into multiple meals: mainly soups. I was content to eat less than I was used to eating. I reaped one great benefit: moderate weight loss. No problem! I will live!

The Ultimatum

After being with Nancy for three weeks, I realized my being in her space was preventing her from living comfortably. Both of us wanted this to end. I was extremely grateful to her for taking me, a complete stranger, into her home, so I did not want to do anything to hurt or offend her in any way.

I told her to put a limit to my stay. She was reluctant to do this. She reminded me I was elderly, broke, unemployed and unknown in Hong Kong. She said that she could not give me an ultimatum to leave soon since I knew no one else in Hong Kong. I insisted on a limit to my stay with her. She relented and gave me a month to leave her place.

"That is too long." I told her.

"A month is too long?" She sounded puzzled.

"Yes. Make it two weeks."

I felt confident I would not need to stay longer. Nancy was troubled for me. She told me, with tears, she would not have left her country with twenty dollars and go to a strange place where she knew no one. She said that called for a level of faith, which she never had although she had previously, "Tried Christianity"

After Nancy agreed to limit my stay to only two more weeks, I felt I wanted to vacate her bedroom before my stay ended. I told her I would sleep on the floor. So she could have her bed back. Since my arrival, Nancy had been sleeping on a futon in the second bedroom, which she had set up for her office. I felt it was time she resumed sleeping on her bed.

She disagreed with me. Again, she cited my elderliness and said that she had to respect me as a guest in her home. I told her it would have been perfectly fine for me to sleep on the floor. This was NOT new to me. She kept silent, and I interpreted this as her consent for me to sleep on her floor. I was WRONG.

"Inventing" a Mattress

Nancy's floor was beautiful, genuine hardwood. They were shiny but cool. I would need a mattress or some pad to cushion my body.

I had a large piece of Scottish plaid material, which my friend Ber in London had sent me. I do not know why I had brought it with me to Hong Kong, but I was glad I had. I decided to make a "mattress" out of it. When I folded it, lengthwise in two, it was slightly smaller than the size of a twin mattress. Perfect! I used most of my clothes to stuff it. Voilla!!! I did it! I invented a mattress. This provided me with comfort and warmth while I slept on Nancy's beautiful hardwood floor. Life was sweet!!

Nancy was not comfortable with my idea. She did not immediately move back into her bedroom. I was not sure of her reasons. Perhaps, she thought I would shortly abandon my decision to sleep on her floor and return to the bedroom. I had no intentions to abandon my idea.

I believe Nancy had done enough for me by meeting me at the airport; accommodating me in her home; assisting me in revising my resume and introducing me to a person, who led me to my first job in Hong Kong. By any standard of generosity, this was phenomenal! I would no longer inconvenience her. I would continue to sleep on my "fabulous mattress" on her floor until her two weeks ultimatum ended or until a change came for me.

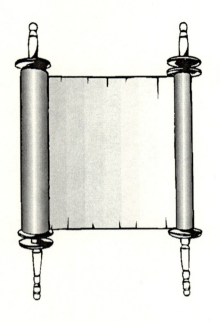

"Could God be calling me out aloud like
He had called Abram?
I was not being facetious. All kinds of weird
thoughts flooded my mind".

6

Who is Calling My Name?

The day after I started sleeping on Nancy's beautiful hardwood floor atop my invented mattress, I went for a walk to the exotic fashion mall nearby. I had been there before to window shop and to use the computer at an Internet café. I liked this mall. I often thought of my daughter Alaya, who is a fashion designer, when I saw the high fashion clothing in many of the prestigious stores.

On this day, soon after entering the mall, I heard my name. I was startled. Who on earth could be calling me? I only knew Nancy, Gabi and her family. I had left Nancy at her home, and I did not know where Gabi and her family were.

Could God be calling me out aloud like He had called Abram? I was not being facetious. All kinds of weird thoughts flooded my mind. Had I unknowingly committed a crime? Did the American Federal Bureau of Investigation (FBI) follow me to Hong Kong from the USA? Who could be calling my name in this large mall, teeming with hundreds of people just a few days after I arrived in Hong Kong?

I stopped. I froze. The call came again. This time, I saw who was calling my name. It was a petite Chinese woman, whom I did not recognize at first. She kept calling, **"Tmay! Tmay! Tmay!"**

She was waving frantically and laughing. I walked toward her. I saw she was Cleo, whom I had met on the airplane from Los Angeles to Hong Kong. I started laughing and waving. We hugged for a long while and laughed heartily. My heart was still pounding with fright, but I was relieved it was **not** the FBI.

Cleo apologized for shouting my name in public. She said she was surprised but happy to see me again. I told her

I was happy to see her, too. She invited me to join her at the Internet Café to have coffee.

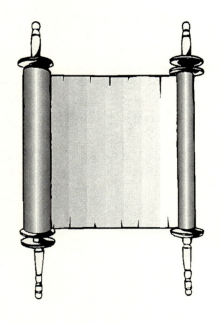

"I was not comparing the two households.

I felt blessed and grateful for what each family

did for me and

for each pre-ordained "upgrade".

7

So Soon?

As we talked, I relaxed. I asked about her son Jae and the rest of her family. She asked me how I was getting along with Nancy. I told her all was well. I also told her of the two – week ultimatum to leave Nancy's home. Cleo then thoroughly shocked me by suggesting I stay at her house for the two weeks or until I found my own place. This seemed unbelievably too soon for my stay at Nancy's to end. I had twelve days remaining in her ultimatum. Besides, I did not ask Cleo for this favor.

I accepted it, and I thanked her. When I returned to Nancy's place and told her of my shopping mall adventure and of Cleo's offer, she, too, was shocked at the early turn of events. I once again thought it was the fruit of my Abrahamic-like faith.

Later, Nancy discovered Cleo's home was a short distance from hers. I could easily walk and wheel my suitcases through the streets from Nancy to Cleo's. No need for a taxi! Wow! Nancy accompanied me there.

My stay at Cleo's was wonderful! I gained two more infant "grandsons." Cleo's family became mine. When I had a serious case of mushroom poisoning, from a gift-meal I ate in a restaurant, Cleo's two helpers nursed me back to health. Magnificent!

Cleo threw a party to celebrate my sixty-first birthday. In addition, on a daily basis, I had more than enough food to eat. I no longer had to split an orange and a banana for three meals. Cleo's family made sure I had all I needed. I was not comparing the two households. I felt blessed and grateful for what each family did for me and for each pre-ordained "upgrade". Praises to Jehovah Jireh!!!!!!! He does provide!

Generous Provisions

Toward the end of my two weeks stay at Cleo's home, my twenty US dollars had dwindled to sixty Hong Kong cents. I prayed for a quick change to my financial need.

An employment opportunity, which Nancy found for me, materialized within a week of my being at Cleo's. With it came housing and a cash advance pending the Hong Kong immigration's endorsement of my business plan. The housing was a large four-bedroom house in the coveted area of Stanley, where tourists to Hong Kong flocked for its white-sand beach and bargain – filled Stanley Market. Unbelievable! I lived in Stanley alone until I met Denise, moved to Discovery Bay and found my own apartment. My housing experience in Hong Kong ran the gamut of sizes. I lived in some of the tiniest and in some of the largest.

Hong Kong had become *"a strong city"* for me. The miracles had begun the moment I met the stranger from Hong Kong in my hotel lobby in Dalian, China. The miracles doubled after I lived in Discovery Bay for a while.

Getting to Hong Kong had appeared improbable initially, but after my first visit, the possibilities of my returning multiplied. Ministry and investment opportunities became realities.

Above all, some of the people of Hong Kong, in and out of the medical industry, were divinely appointed to rescue and save me from death and the unpredictable aftermath of ruptured Brain Aneurysms.

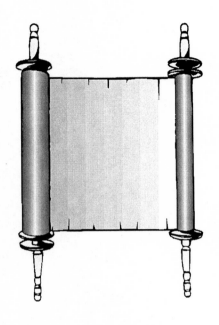

"Then this city shall bring me renown,

joy praise and honor

before all nations on the earth that hear all the

good things I do for it;

…abundant prosperity and peace

I provide for it.

Jeremiah 33: 9"

8

Finding a Jamaican

Hearing about Discovery Bay

I first heard of Discovery Bay, Hong Kong, popularly called **DB,** from a resident, whom I met at a pre-Christmas sale in one of the large hotels on Hong Kong Island in 1999. It did not surprise me she is Jamaican. There is a standard joke: "anywhere in and out of the world one goes, one will find Jamaicans".

This gorgeous Jamaican woman, Denise, had lived in many countries including England, New Zealand, Australia and now Hong Kong. We have had similar travel experiences. We compared travel notes, exchanged contact information and promised to keep in touch.

When we met, Denise was living with her family in Discovery Bay on Lan Tau Island, and I was living alone in Stanley, Hong Kong. I lived within a minute of the beach. I liked the calm, beauty and serenity I experienced when living close to water anywhere. In Stanley, I enjoyed sitting, reading, writing or watching the boats sailing along the horizon. The water skiers meandering closer to the shore fascinated me.

Denise, my new Jamaican friend, said she liked Stanley, so I invited her for lunch. She came on a Saturday. She stopped at the famous "Stanley Market" to get beautiful flowers for herself and for me.

Before and during lunch, we talked about the flowers and cheerfully identified those, which also grew in Jamaica. We reminisced about our love for flowers during our youthful days in Jamaica.

We recalled how even the most modest and most sparsely furnished home in Jamaica had an outside garden and a walkway lined with flowers and framed by whitewashed stones. The house was often adorned within with exotic, cut flowers in beautiful vases or in bottles or tin cans masquerading as decorative vases, especially on the weekends, Christmas, Easter, Independence Day and other significant holidays.

We ate lunch. The avocado, sweet potatoes and pink snapper also reminded us of Jamaica. We thought; all we needed were some sweet potato pudding, ginger beer or sorrel, to complete the feast. We sang in Jamaican Patois the song: **"Dis lang time gal mi neva see yuh!"** (The standard English could be: This long time girl, I never see you, or it is a long time since I have seen you girl!) We laughed hilariously as we sang and enjoyed our time together.

After lunch, we cleaned up the kitchen, and went for a walk along Stanley beach. It was more like going for a "sat" on the beach. Both of us were too full to walk. We sat near the water under a canopy and watched the more agile adults and youth prancing up and down the beach and the water skiers whisking by. We enjoyed the flowers; our "labrish"

(Louise Bennett), our luncheon and our attempted walk along the beach. What could have topped that?

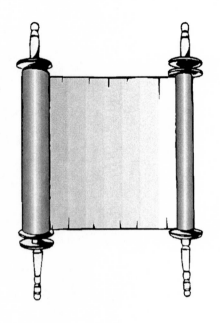

"The moment I got there,

I knew I had "discovered' the place

I wanted to call "home" for a long time.

Discovery Bay captured my heart and became

my city of joy".

9

Making DB My Home

Afew weekends later, Denise invited me to visit her family in Discovery Bay. To get there, I traveled by bus from Stanley then by ferry from Central on the large Hong Kong Island to Lan Tau Island. The trip was exciting! I had walked on the beach in Stanley, but here I was sailing on the waters surrounding Lau Tau Island on which DB is located. The moment I got there, I knew I had "discovered' the place I wanted to call "home" for a long time.

Discovery Bay captured my heart and became my "city of joy". After returning to Stanley, I thought constantly of DB, where I had at least one friend. In Stanley I had none.

I was thinking of how to make DB my home. Shortly after my first visit to DB, the conditions, which lead me to Stanley, began changing. Eventually, I would have to move. I told my friend of my desire to move to Discovery Bay. She thought it was a good idea, and she offered her assistance. She allowed me to vacation with her family for two weeks.

Within this time, I found a flat to share with someone for part of the rent and the utilities. After two months of sharing, I found a place of my own. It was on the fifteenth floor of a high rise overlooking the bay. The view was spectacular. The large French windows made it seem as if the flowers and trees outside were giant, framed wall hangings in my bedrooms and living room. The outdoors became a part of my interior décor. Nature was my interior designer.

The Best Landlord

My Chinese landlord, Rick, was quite interesting. He is man of deep faith and an agriculturist. He specializes in the science of cultivating Marigold from which scientists extract Lutein, a key ingredient in protective eye care products and the natural yellow coloring for margarine and other foods. Rick was sub-letting his apartment in order to move to China to supervise the farming of Marigold. I felt honored to have met Rick and to be the temporary inheritor of all his wonderful books on Christianity, Agriculture and many other subjects.

In addition to his personal library, he furnished the apartment tastefully and included <u>all</u> the household appliances, which would simplify my daily living. He even provided some electronic equipment he thought I would have needed for my professional work and for entertainment.

He instructed me on living economically and made his contribution by charging me a reasonable rent for excellent living conditions. He was the most considerate landlord I have had in my renting history. I owe him more than a huge debt of gratitude. I owe him a double debt of love and honor. I pray he and I will meet again.

The panoramic view from my fifteenth floor window seemed familiar. The flattened point of the hill jutting out in the bay is similar to the two ends of Jamaica jutting out in the Caribbean Sea. By Day and by night I watched the boats going back and forth from DB to Peng Chau, a small island, about ten minutes away from DB. I also watched the First Ferries en route to Mui Wo at the far end of Lan Tau Island.

Once or twice weekly, I went to Peng Chau to shop for fresh fruits, vegetables and flowers. I often visited the post office and library, did my laundry, exercised, or dined alone or with friends.

The highlight of my weekly visits to Pen Chau was to watch the fishers, men and women, empty their boats of the fish they had caught. I was always amazed at how they kept most of the fish alive for display in the built – in ponds on the floor of the small fish market. This makes it easy for shoppers to identify the fish they want, as they swim around, and select them for their meal. They could get fish no fresher than this!

Topping Stanley

Living in Discovery Bay topped living in Stanley for me. Perhaps, it is because of the excellent housing; the low pollution levels; the floral beauty of the surroundings; the international diversities of the residents and the ease of traveling to anywhere. May be it is because DB felt more like home to me. There is also a Discovery Bay in my homeland Jamaica in the Caribbean that embodies similar qualities.

Like Discovery Bay, Jamaica, Discovery Bay, Hong Kong has an, *"I welcome you, and I don't want you to leave" atmosphere.*

I found it difficult to leave DB once I got there. I had to leave twice to care for my ill mother Mabelle, who was living either in Jamaica or in the USA. I HAD to return. Each time I returned to either of the Discovery Bays - Jamaica's or Hong Kong's, the feeling of being at home quickly returns and lasts well beyond the duration of the visits.

The spirit of the miraculous is resident in both Discovery Bays. This spirit became a personal reality for me when I experienced two miracles, sixty-nine days apart while living in Discovery Bay, Hong Kong in the year 2002.

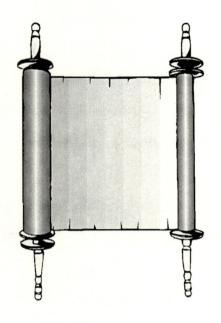

"Hearing Jordan's joyful sounds, his laughter
and seeing his "crocodile" tears,
rejuvenated me and reminded me of the days
when my three children's joyful sounds, laughter
and "crocodile" tears were the reasons for my
existence".

10

Before The First Miracle: Part I

Home Away From Home

Since 1999, I called Discovery Bay, Hong Kong home. Being part of an island, it reminded me of the Discovery Bay in my exotic Caribbean nation, Jamaica. From my windows in Hong Kong's DB, I could see a hill, which indents into a gooseneck shape like parts of Jamaica. On days when I felt nostalgic, I would gaze at the sights of trees, shrubs and flowers and ocean and hear the sound of the waves, like galloping horses, washing over the huge boulders and crashing against the retaining walls of the small pier adjacent to my home.

I am always fascinated by the galloping "white horses" (Campbell). In my childish reverie, I often wondered which "horse" won as the foaming waves rejoin the watery course.

I could see boats of various kinds anchored and others sailing back and forth to Peng Chau and other nearby destinations. The view was ironically comforting and disturbing since the nostalgia caused me to be happy but to also long for and even pine for my native Jamaica.

I kept busy by getting involved in church's ministry and the life of the community.

A Gift of Time

I gave Alaya, one of my daughters, a *"gift of time"* to care for her son when she started having childcare problems in New York. My first grandson Jordan, who was turning five, came to spend summer 2000 with me. He loved Discovery Bay. He asked to stay longer. Alaya agreed, and I extended my **"gift of time"** to one year. He lived in DB with me for eight months.

He was a rare gift to me. He arrived just when I was feeling an acute need for companionship. Despite warnings about caring for such a young, energetic a child at my age of sixty-two years, I found it only slightly challenging to care for Jordan. It was over twenty years since I had cared for his mother. I had to learn to listen more attentively to him.

I tried to be a caring and amusing grandma while maintaining a healthy balance between levity and discipline. Hearing Jordan's joyful sounds, his laughter and seeing his "crocodile" tears, rejuvenated and reminded me of the days when my three children's joyful sounds, laughter and "crocodile" tears were the reasons for my existence. Jordan had a huge sense of humor for his small size and tender years. It was so rich in innocence and creativity. I had teases and tricks, which intrigued, mesmerized and even taunted him. **We had fun!**

We laughed constantly. Next to our daily devotions and Bible study, our Saturday morning pillow fights were the crowning feature of our week. It was deliberating for me to jump up and down on my bed and pound Jordan with pillow after pillow. He would return the "favor" with all his might. We laughed, pounced on each other, tussled, and rolled like two little pigs enjoying a mud bath. WHEEEEEEEEEEEEE!!!!!!!!!!!!

Although we do it less often now, as he approaches pre-teen, we still enjoy a rousing round of pillow fight. We have more cushions and pillows to throw at each other.

Sponge Bob, Elmo, Care Bear, Daffy Duck, Mickey Mouse, snakes and zillions of other stuffed toys have joined our arsenal. We still have major fun. WOW!!!!!!!!!!!!!!!!!!!!!!

Having Jordan with me in Discovery Bay at that time, opened avenues of friendships with other parents and guardians with whom I arranged play dates between their children and Jordan. The parents and I took turns organizing play dates in the mornings and afternoons during the week and having sleepovers and boating trips on weekends.

The period of eight months, which Jordan spent with me in DB, was one of much learning and adventures for both of us. The stories could fill several books. Among the highlights for Jordan, were the three celebrations of his fifth birth date, one in Peng Chau, one in Discovery Bay and one in Beijing.

Our twenty-nine hour train trip to Beijing, our trip to Dang Dong and our short- term mission trip to Thailand were among the most memorable events. To complete the year's gift of time, we spent three months in Fort Lauderdale Florida and one month in Jamaica. Jordan traveled well. We lived happily.

Jordan has become a brilliant young man, budding musician and professional model. His advanced communication skills allow him to articulate his views on any subject and to converse easily with both children and adults.

My second Grandson Miles Kingsley Discuillo, who also gives me permission to include him in my book, was born to my first daughter Jessica on September 02, 1999, while I was in Discovery Bay.

Although he is three years younger than Jordan, I wished he could have been with us in DB. It would have been double the fun and would have added another pleasant dimension to my life as a proud grand mother of two lovely boys then.

I had to be content with speaking with Miles by phone and through letters. This too, was fun since Miles was brilliant for his age and quite humorous, too. I enjoyed hearing his detailed descriptions of all fifty states and receiving his cleverly decorated original cards and letters. He amazed me!

Miles, at eight years of age, has become quite a dancer. He had his debut in summer 2007 and a major part in "The Nut Cracker" in winter 2007. He is FUNNY!!!!

He has adopted my childhood nickname- "Fox tail" as his.

Both Jordan and Miles gave me great bragging rights. Now I have three. Micah, Jordan's brother, who is presently a toddler and a potential great pillow fighter, doctor and artist, is adding more. Since he cannot give me his permission to include him in my book, I will not say more about this adorable, darling. He will be the main character in the book "Helper". They all give me bragging rights. **I am a proud Nana!**

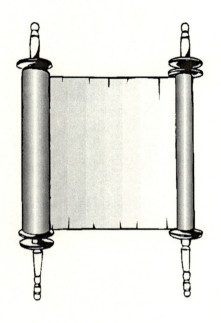

"It was exceptionally soothing to have these
encouraging words from someone who cares
as I am weathering the storm of
my mother's illness;
natural storms and my personal, disquieting
storms of unresolved issues".

11

Before The First Miracle: Part II

Caring for Mother

One event that added a troubling dimension to my stay in Hong Kong was my mother's illness. Mabelle had lived in Jamaica at the time. Since I was the unofficial, designated caregiver among her three children, this prompted my departure from Hong Kong to care for her. It meant leaving my newly endorsed sole proprietorship business as an education consultant and family educator twice. The second time was an unexpected, extended leave of nineteen months from my business and from Discovery Bay.

When my mother was sufficiently recovered, I traveled with her from Fort Lauderdale, Florida, where I had taken her for medical attention, back to her home in Jamaica. I was now free to return to Hong Kong to continue living in Discovery Bay and to restart my business if the Hong Kong Immigration Department gave me a second endorsement.

I returned to Hong Kong on Miles' third birth date – September 02, 2002.

The Stormy Welcome

A typhoon was raging over Taiwan when I was returning, and we could feel the effects of it in the turbulent air as we approached Hong Kong. The pilots turned on the "Fasten Seat Belt" sign and warned us of a bumpy ride.

Smoothest Landing

Despite this warning of a bumpy ride, they succeeded in minimizing the effects of the rough air and eventually achieved the smoothest landing of a jumbo 747 I have ever experienced in my entire flying history as a passenger. It were as if some super, strong arms had taken the huge Cathay Pacific aircraft and gently set it down on the tarmac. "Planediferous"!!

Welcome Back!

As soon as we landed at Hong Kong's mega airport, I felt I was home. From my arrival at the airport, I started to see familiar faces. One of the pilots, who brought us safely through the turbulence, was my neighbor. We chit - chatted about our families and exchanged hugs. I spoke with two other pilots. I asked them who was "guilty" of such a smooth landing. Each "blamed" the other. Everyone, who heard our jiving, laughed and thanked then.

I looked forward to returning to Discovery Bay and to my apartment in Haven in Haven Court. My extended leave made me realize how much I *liked living there and how much I loved the people.* "Absence makes the heart grow fonder" was true for me.

Several days after arriving in DB, I saw more neighbors and friends. They all expressed how much they had missed me and how pleased they were I had returned. The outpouring of friendly sentiments was reassuring for me. I did not think I had impacted anyone's life, during the two years I had lived in DB, prior to leaving my new business to care for my mother.

I thought differently when a few days after I returned to DB, someone sent me a beautifully handcrafted card with these words:

"I am glad the Lord brought you back to Hong Kong, so that I might get to know you. Your faith and joy in the Lord is an inspiration to me, and I believe that even when you are gone, your life will continue to challenge me to new heights in Him. May God bless you in the days to come as you discover the next steps in His great plan for you. With love..."JC

It was exceptionally soothing to have these encouraging words from someone who cares as I was weathering the storm of my mother's illness; natural storms and my personal disquieting storms of unresolved issues.

I had to wait for my apartment to be vacant. Kind friends provided temporary accommodations for over a week. I passed the time by reading, writing, meditating and hiking.

Water From Heaven

On September 15, 2002, I turned sixty-four. Early in the morning, I took an extended power prayer walk up the hill toward the Discovery Bay golf course. It rained. I love walking in the rain.

It reminded me of my childhood in rural Jamaica. It was often necessary to walk miles to school, church, market, the post office and grocery store during a drenching rain, bare footed. Then the children had no choice about going out in the rain. We were told to go and we went. I liked getting soaked to my bones, and I still like getting soaked as a senior adult. It is so refreshing and invigorating!

On my sixty-fourth birth date, I welcomed the rain as a cleansing, rejuvenating washing by a heavenly shower. Before going on my prayer walk, I prepared hot water with lemon wedges to drink after warming up with stretches and a leisurely walk, as usual. I drank the brew then put the empty mug on my head. Of course, I was a spectacle to curious onlookers.

I was not seeking attention. I needed to free my hands, and my head became my second set of hands. I acquired this skill in my childhood from carrying buckets of water and baskets loaded with colorful fruits and vegetables on my head. I thought the rain was great. I could catch water in my mug. I did just that. The rain fell into my mug as I walked up the hill.

Later, I poured it in an attractive bottle as a birthday present to me from above. I called it, "Water from Heaven".

During my walk, I met several people. One was Linda, the wife of one of the many pilots, who lived in Discovery Bay. We chatted pleasantly in the drenching rain. I told her of my intent to write to President George Bush about the conflict with Iraq. She said it was a great idea, and she thought her husband Michael might also have an interest in writing.

I was excited at the prospect of joining with others to communicate with President George W. Bush. Over the next few days, I prayed, watched the news and wondered what I might say to President Bush.

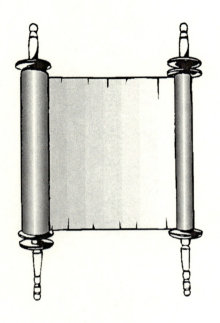

"For you, o Lord, have delivered my soul from

death

My eyes from tears

And my feet from stumbling

That I may walk before the Lord

In the land of the living

Psalm 116: 8-9 NIV"

12

The First Miracle

Three Women Prayed

On Thursday, September 19, 2002, Jacinth, Jenna and I gathered in the "Greens", one of the luxurious high-rise apartment dwellings, in Discovery Bay. We usually pray weekly on a Friday, but this week was the exception; we gathered on a Thursday.

Three events etched this date in my memory permanently. It was eight days after the painful first anniversary of the dreadful attack on the World Trade Center in New York. It was the birth date of the "First Lady" of our congregation, and I had planned to honor her after our gathering. It was exactly two weeks after my return from an extended leave from Discovery Bay to care for my then ailing, mother in Jamaica and the United States.

The one o'clock weekly gathering of the women to pray was for me a time of renewal. It was an opportunity to pray with others for common concerns. One of our concerns was for families in DB, Hong Kong and the rest of the world. Another major concern was for the political tension between the United States and Iraq. Since multi-cultural groups live in Hong Kong and in DB, many countries were mentioned in our prayers. We gathered to pray for resolution to world – wide economic, environmental, political, spiritual and social issues and those affecting us in DB and Hong Kong

I arrived in the Greens at Jacinth's home, the venue for our gathering, shortly before one o'clock in the after noon. Jenna had called to say she was on her way. She came within a few minutes of her call. The three of us chatted briefly, and Jacinth and Jenna selected a CD of contemporary Christian music.

When the music started, we stopped talking and listened intently to the music as we prepared to pray. The music ushered in a tranquil atmosphere, and we responded with a focused discussion of prayer needs for the world, Hong Kong, DB and ourselves. Jacinth divided the various issues among the three of us, so each woman had several issues for which to pray.

We prayed silently first to prepare individually and pray for our unspoken needs. We then prayed in round-robin- style, beginning with praises, until we had addressed all the voiced issues. Each of us prayed several times. I distinctly recall the joy of our fellowship and the unity of our prayer. We remembered the promise to the "two or three", so we were not concerned about being few in number. By our "mustard seed" faith, and the power of prayer, we could move the mountains of social injustice, poverty, famine, wars, geno-cide, political conflicts and other ills.

I also recall clearly, I was seated between Jenna on my left and Jacinth on my right. After our period of silent prayer, Jenna prayed aloud for some of the issues Jacinth assigned her. When she finished praying, I asked Jenna and Jacinth to stand with me for the symbolic defeat of Lucifer.

I believe Lucifer, also called, Satan, devil, old serpent dragon evil one, is real. As believers, we have the power to cause him to flee and defeat him at his game to "…devour whom he may" (I Peter 5:8) By being devoted and obedient to God, a believer can resist and rebuke the evil one *and he will flee* (James 4:7).

The scripture empowers us to "… tread upon the lion and adder: the young lion and the dragon shall you trample under your feet. (Psalm 91: 13). This was the scriptural motivation for my inviting Jenna and Jacinth to join with me and symbolically trample Lucifer under our feet.

A Quick Reassurance

Recently, one of my Chinese sisters asked me about the association of one of Chinese cultural icons, the dragon, with the devil. She was concerned about the possibility of having to abandon her enjoyment of cultural activities related to the dragon.

I hasten to say I do not believe the Chinese cultural icon the dragon is synonymous with Lucifer. The words, "Dragon, serpent, adder, roaring lion, Father of Lies, Prince of the Air" and others, are metaphors for Satan. There is absolutely no need to abandon activities such as watching a live "Dragon Boat Race" or to stop watching the fictional television characters "Lion King" and "Flying Dragon".

In both my childhood and adult experiences, I learned about the tremendous power of prayer from Holy Scriptures and from writings such as Corrie Tem Boom's. I quote her. "More is wrought by prayers than this world dreams of". This truth supports the power of praying regularly instead of despairing.

Gathering to pray with others was always a gift to me, but I did not expect to receive the precious gift of a miracle four days after my sixty-fourth birth date. I was the receiver not the witness of the miracle, so I am unable to recount all of it in my own words. It was as if I were "absent" from some of the scenes.

We expected answers to our prayers and even miracles, but none of us could predict September 19, 2002 would be the date of the first of the double miracles I would experience in Discovery Bay, Hong Kong. Jacinth and Jenna's reports, and the testimonies of others, were sufficient to convince me of the first, great life saving miracle I received.

This was also confirmed sixty-nine days later when the second medical emergency occurred. I was admitted to Princess Margaret Hospital with the worst headache of my life. I had brain surgery. The surgeons, who performed the craniotomy, said the presence of dried blood showed I had a previous bleeding. After I returned to America, the neurologist at Columbia Presbyterian Hospital called it a "sentinel bleed." It was a warning something was terribly wrong in my brain.

The bleed had caused me to faint, "black out" and to become totally unaware of myself and of everything. No one at the gathering or in my apartment knew what had happened to me. Although I might have appeared well to others, my brain was functioning in a way that made me unaware of what I was doing.

Regrettably, I did not heed the warning of the "sentinel bleed". I should have gone to the doctor as soon as was possible after I had fainted for a check up. The appropriate tests would have revealed what took place in my brain on September 19, 2002, and detect developing aneurysms. Because I felt well for sixty-nine days, I made the serious mistake of ignoring the clear warning. I did not see a doctor.

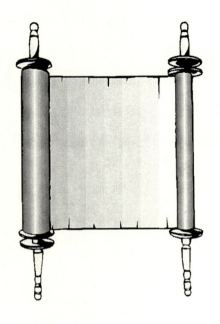

"I believed I walked, but I was unaware of it.

I was like a dead woman walking with live

people.

I am not sure how many.

I knew of only two before I fainted".

13

Dead Woman Walked

Totally Unaware

This sounds ironic, but I have no other way of expressing what happened after I fainted. I cannot recall what actually happened between one o'clock in the afternoon and ten o'clock at night of September 19th, 2002, after I "blacked out" in the prayer gathering in the Greens of DB. I saw nothing or no one although there were people with me. I felt nothing. Someone must have lifted me from the floor. I heard nothing. Jacinth and Jenna, who were with me, must have talked, called my name or did some thing to try and revive me. Try as I may, I cannot recall the events of more than nine hours between the prayer gathering at one o'clock in the afternoon and my return to the Greens at ten thirty at night

I believed I walked, but I was unaware of it. I was like a dead woman walking with live people. I am not sure how many. I knew of only two before I fainted.

Bus Stop Flashback

At around ten o'clock at night, while standing at the bus stop in DB Plaza with Jacinth and her husband Coleman, I suddenly realized I was standing at the same bus stop, where I had stood approximately nine and a half hours before, to travel to the Greens for the prayer gathering during daylight. It was now night. The gathering must have ended, so why was I still at the bus stop? I had no clue, so I asked the obvious.

"What am I doing here?"

"Well, we took you back to your apartment and you did not seem to know where you were, so we are taking you back to our house."

I tried to figure out why anyone would have to take me back to my apartment, when I was quite capable of going there by myself. How could I have gone there and not know it? What had happened in the Greens to cause my friends to take me back to my place? What happened at my place? Why am I returning, escorted by them to the Greens? My silence spoke so loudly, Jacinth and Coleman answered.

"You blacked out while praying at our house, and we took you back to your place."

"You took me back to my apartment?" I did not know I was there. I did not see it or see me there. I saw no one. I was shocked.

"Well, you were there and other people were there."

"Who?" I asked.

"Pastor was there…" She rattled off a long list of names while my amazement grew into a mountain.

"I did not see them. I saw no one." I said so firmly.

I kept silent again wondering and pondering how could I have been so blind not to have seen I was taken back to my apartment, and once I got there, how did I not see anything or anyone! I was just silently wondering what I did or said during the nine hours I was totally unaware of everything, when the bus arrived.

Everything was such a mystery to me. I kept silent for the rest of the trip to the Greens. I was still dazed as if some gigantic, unknown thing had hit me. Keeping silent brought calm and energy. I wondered, "What is going on?" "What will happen next?"

Ground Omega

We arrived back on familiar ground. This was where it all began. I surveyed the living room where Jacinth, Jenna and I had gathered. I sat again in the French window overlooking the bay. The view was spectacular. Shimmering lights danced on the water of Discovery Bay. The white boats, creeping in on the dark water made a powerful contrast in the night. "White horses" (George Campbell) raced on both sides and in front of the ferryboats and crashed on the restraining wooden barriers and concrete walls.

As I sat, I looked for clues to jog my memory. I found none. I closed my eyes; I tried to recapture the scene before the prayer gathering, which ended abruptly for the three of us and almost fatally for me. I could recall the inspirational praise music and the serenity of the moment. I recalled

Jenna's prayer. I also recalled inviting Jenna and Jacinth to stand with me and to symbolically trample Lucifer.

I recalled that we stood. I held hands with Jenna on my left and with Jacinth on my right. That is all I can recall. It was as if at that moment someone closed a heavy curtain and the stage darkened. I cannot recall trampling Lucifer. I cannot recall fainting. I cannot recall falling.

When Coleman and Jacinth escorted me back to their home, I sensed I was there before, but I was still wondering why I was returning at night. I was totally confused, stupefied and famished.

My reminiscing ended when Jacinth returned to tell me a room was ready for me. She showed me to the room and told me to make myself at home. I thanked her, but I thought why couldn't I be at home in my place? My mind was still drawing blanks.

Coleman and Jacinth fixed a light, hot supper. They talked while we ate. I was famished, so I kept quiet as my mind wandered. When our nightcap ended, I helped to clean up. The three of us sat talking for a few minutes.

Whose names?

Suddenly, Jacinth called some names and asked me, "Who are these people"?

Hearing those names startled me. I did not recall saying those names. I was concerned about what secrets or private matters I might have revealed.

"Oh! Where did you hear those names? How did you get those names"?

Jacinth explained. "When you were back at your place, you did a lot of things".

"Oh! Oh! This sounds horrible"; I thought. "Like what?" I asked uneasily.

"You talked a lot about your husband. You called his name over and over, and you called these names, too. You cried. You laughed. You sang. You danced. You prayed."

I was troubled to hear this since I could not remember being back in my apartment much more doing all those things. I recalled stopping my ears, when Jacinth spoke, but I did not explain who the people were.

I wondered why I called those particular names. Jacinth's chronicle of my behavior seemed incomplete, so I asked expectantly, "What else did I say? What more did I do?" Jacinth answered in a matter- of- fact way, "Some things are better kept unsaid".

I had learned this maxim earlier in my life. It was good advice then. It was good advice on this day and night of mysteries. I calmed my mind and accepted the unknown over which I had no control. We spoke for a few more minutes then the three of us retired for the night. I slept well, but did not dream. I rose early, as it was my custom, to exercise, pray, meditate and write.

My hosts were pleased I enjoyed my first night in their home, especially after a dramatic and traumatic happening earlier in the day. I awoke still wishing I could have remembered what happened. I encountered many temptations to revisit the happenings of the previous day and to ask Coleman and Jacinth many questions. I resisted the temptations. I asked no questions and they volunteered no information.

"Mum" was the motto of the moment.

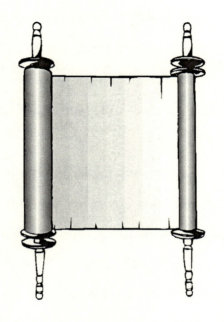

"…His compassions fail not.

They are new every morning.

Great is Your Faithfulness

Lamentations 3:15"

14

New Feelings

Bus Stop Realization

From the time I found myself at the bus stop the day before, more than nine hours after the prayer gathering had ended, I noticed there was a difference about my feelings in both my mind and body. I felt lighter and suspended as if I were hanging between two worlds – a little out in space, but not spaced out. I felt calm within, but unlike the days preceding my blacking out, I did not feel grounded.

It was now September 21, 2002. I could recall most of the events of days, weeks, months and even years prior to September 19, 2002. My short-term memory of some of the happenings in Jacinth's home and all of the occurrences in my apartment on the day I fainted, were completely erased.

Days of Reflection

During my two-day stay at Jacinth's home, I became more aware of people, places, things and myself. I had chances to relax completely; however, I felt here, the scene of the first miracle, was the ideal setting in which to finish what I started to prepare for the fall semester.

My first plan was to complete the paperwork for my investment visa and to contact the Hong Kong Immigration Department. My second plan was to contact the university, where I expected to serve as an education consultant, and make an appointment to meet with the dean. My third plan was to meet and work with Michael, the pilot, whose wife I had met on my sixty-fourth birth date, to write to President George Bush.

In addition to the letter the pilot and I would write, I would also write a personal letter to President Bush. Jacinth allowed me to use her computer and assisted me in setting it up to write the letters. I wrote to President George Bush, and

I drafted another letter with the intent to work with Michael to make it a petition from the Discovery Bay Community

At the end of my two- day stay with Jacinth and Coleman, they graciously escorted me my back to my apartment. This time I understood why, and I appreciated their escort. I valued their hospitality; their care and their concern for my well - being. They brought with them, to my apartment, household and grocery items they thought I needed. They remained for several hours to help me initiate my resettlement.

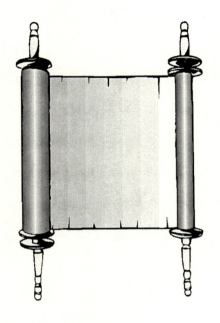

"Without fully realizing what had caused me to

faint in the prayer meeting,

they had become eyewitnesses to a miracle and

key players in its reality".

15

Alive Again!

Soon after I became aware of being alive, I had a feeling much more had happened to me than I would ever know or needed to know. I also felt all who were present in the Greens, where we prayed and in Haven Court, where I lived, did more for my survival than I could ever imagine. I also believed they, too, were traumatized unknowingly. The old maxim says, "What you don't know, doesn't hurt." This is not necessarily always true although it has an element of protection.

I believe my friends in DB lovingly and responsibly protected me from myself and whatever else was present.

Without fully realizing what had caused me to faint in the prayer meeting, they had become eyewitnesses to a miracle and key players in its reality. An aneurysm had ruptured in my brain. This caused me to black out and lose awareness. Because of the serious nature of any aneurysm rupturing, I could have easily died instantly or within the nine hours when I was totally unaware.

I have overcome my guilt of the indignities and difficulties to which I might have unknowingly subjected my friends, and I have replaced that guilt with eternal gratitude. They prayed. They cared. They rescued a "walking dead" woman. Now I can shout: I AM ALIVE AGAIN!!!!!!!!!!!!

Oversized blessings await everyone who helped me when I fainted on September 19, 2002. Although I walked as a dead woman, their prayers moved the Great Physician to restore my life. I pray their lives will change in positive and remarkable ways as a reward for helping me.

WHAT A MIRACLE!

After I returned to my apartment in Haven Court several persons visited me. All expressed joy at seeing me again.

Jakes was both joyful and amazed. He said he believed it was a miracle I was alive. He said he came to my apartment after Jacinth and Jenna escorted me back from the Greens after the prayer gathering, He explained how I looked color-less and how my eyes rolled back in their sockets. "We saw death written all over you."

This sent chills up and down my spine as he talked. I felt foolish because I still did not grasp the full gravity of the situation as he explained it to me. It was as if I were not there when it happened. I was totally unaware of what took place in my apartment on the afternoon and evening of September 19, 2002.

I closed my eyes as he spoke and tried to recapture the scene and to recall seeing Jakes and the others who were there. I came up empty. Jakes spoke again firmly,

"It is a miracle; I tell you. We saw death written all over you, and we prayed. We just kept praying and praying"

"Thank you for praying for me. I thank all of you".

I thanked them for praying although I still did not fully grasp the extent of their actions and the gravity of my problem.

"Don't thank us. Thank God. Only God could have done this. Only He could have brought you back." As he spoke, those present agreed with him.

Another spoke. "Yes, it is a miracle. Thank God you made it."

I was still dazed by the talk of my near-death experience of which I was totally unaware. It occurred to me they were confirming a miracle, and they were unaware I did not fully understand them. Because I was conscious, talkative, tearful, mobile and even rambunctious, when I had amnesia, they might have thought I knew what I was doing. I wish I did. I would have spared them some of the indignities to which I might have subjected them. **The depth of my gratitude for what they did underscores the power of friendship, love and prayer. Through these three elements they preserved my life to tell of the miraculous.**

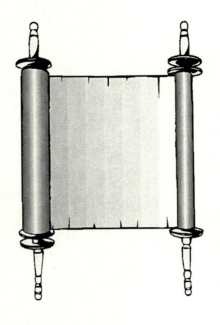

"Is any sick among you? Let him call for the

elders of the church;

and let them pray over him...."

(James 5:14)

16

Active Faith

Following "The Leader"

It is more than amazing, from a human perspective, that without medical intervention I survived the first ruptured brain aneurysm. Each time I would verbally tell the story of the first miracle, someone would ask the same question: "Did you call the paramedics?" When I said I could not, the person would ask, "Did anyone else call?"

My answer is always the same: "I do not know. I am not sure."

I sensed no one had called the emergency medical service; otherwise, I would have been taken to a doctor's office or to a hospital. I was taken back to my apartment and then back to Jacinth's home. Because of my deep gratitude for the actions, which saved my life, I have never questioned if anyone called the paramedics. I address the subject here, to answer those, who have asked and others, who will be asking.

I have no intent to cast doubt or to suggest any impropriety or indiscretion on the actions of my friends and rescuers. I remain eternally grateful for their care, love and prayers.

I believe they unleashed their strong faith and did according to the Holy Scriptures: *"Is any sick among you? Let him call for the elders of the church, and let them pray over him anointing him with oil in the name of the Lord: And **the prayer of faith shall save the sick, and the Lord shall raise him up....**" James 5: 14-15* (Emphasis mine)

It is my firm belief they would have prayed whether or not they had called the paramedics. Only God performs true miracles, and it requires one to exercise strong faith for a true miracle to materialize. On my behalf, they put action to their faith and called on God, who "…neither slumbers nor sleeps…." (Psalm 121:3-4 KJV) He answered them.

Their actions do not preclude or suggest not calling for emergency medical help if someone faints for no apparent reason. Those present at an emergency must exercise wisdom and informed judgment on behalf of the person they are helping. I believe all my rescuers did just that.

Again, I register my profound and eternal gratitude for the actions of everyone, who was there when I "was not". I appreciate your obedience to the Holy Spirit, who led you to, "…keep praying". I thank you with my whole heart.

You were pre-ordained to perform a phenomenal act of love, FAITH and courage to rescue me from death.

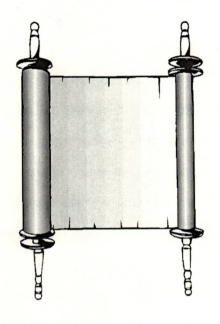

"He will swallow up death into victory…"

Isaiah 25:8

17

Sixty- nine Days Death Free

Counting from September 19, 2002, when the first miracle happened to November 24, 2002, the date of the second miracle, is exactly sixty-nine days. I call this the "death free" period. Working with Michael and Linda to write a letter to President George Bush was one of the most productive things I did during this period. It was not writing to President Bush, per se that made it productive, but it was the fact I was able to recall events prior to **my blackout and nine hours of amnesia.**

Days of Reflection

While at Coleman and Jacinth's home, I remembered walking in the rain, with a mug on my head up the hill in Discovery Bay, on my sixty-fourth birth date. I remembered speaking with Linda, the pilot's wife, about writing to President George Bush. I was pleased I remembered so much since I had forgotten most of what happened to me on September 19, 2002. I decided to follow my intention to join with others to write to President George W. Bush about the American- Iraqi conflict.

Michael and Linda liked the idea of writing a letter then making it a petition from the many people from other countries, who were living in Discovery Bay if they agreed. They would have the option to signify their countries stance or their own opinions. I met with Linda and Michael in their home, and we discussed the matter. Together, we drafted the letter. With their permission, I reprint it at the end of this chapter.

The responsibility to gather signatures was mine. For two days, I walked through the Discovery Bay Plaza at various hours when crowds of people gathered to recreate, dine, shop or just hang out. I presented the letter with a brief verbal introduction and invited people to read and sign if they wished.

Everyone read the petition, but not everyone signed it. Some of those, who refused to sign, strongly voice their reason and their anger at the American's stance against Iraq. In two days, I collected more than three hundred signatures. The popular opinion of some of the signatories was, "We will get no response from President Bush or his staff." We did not let the possibility of no response deter us. I mailed the letter to President Bush.

It was important to let President Bush know we cared. We had an opinion about the American-Iraq conflict, and were voicing it. We felt in the end it mattered whether we kept silent or voiced our opinion despite what America under President Bush's leadership decided to do in Iraq.

The South China Morning Post featured this headline seven days before we mailed our letter: "Iraq says No to

Bush's Demands." We wanted to stand with the President as he considered a just cause of action.

LETTER TO PRESIDENT GEORGE W. BUSH:

Concerned World Citizens

Discovery Bay, Lantau Island

HONG KONG, PEOPLE'S REPUBLIC OF CHINA

September 21, 2002

President George W. Bush

The President of the United States of America

The White House

Pennsylvania Avenue

Washington, D.C. 20002

UNITED STATES OF AMERICA

Dear President Bush:

Re: The Iraqi Issue.

We write to you as concerned world citizens from a diverse and varied cultural grouping in Discovery Bay, Hong Kong. We find ourselves as one in our views and desires in the conduct of constraint upon Saddam Hussein and his efforts to destabilize world security.

Collectively, we state the following:

We recognize that the mantle of leadership and responsibility that you have chosen to shoulder in becoming the President of the United States of America is a burden of the highest demand. This burden is increased greatly because the interdependence of this Modern world is such that your constituency is not limited to that of the American people as it once was for those who preceded you in simpler times. This wider world constituency is largely supportive of all that the United States of America stands for, but it desires to be fully involved and included in the process of world governance.

We believe that the constraints upon the Iraqi leadership, that you are so vigorous in pursuing, are undoubtedly required; however, much of the moral validity that your government presently enjoys on this issue could be jeopardized through any unilateral conduct of action. Whilst time is no doubt a precious resource, so is unity of purpose and collective will.

We call on you and your administration to maintain a collective approach in the prosecution of Iraqi activities that are contrary to United Nations Security Council resolutions and to continue to do so exclusively under the legal framework of the United Nations Charter.

In closing let us remember the words of Winston Churchill in addressing the British Parliament on May 13th 1940; "Come then, let us go forward together with our united strength."

We the undersigned concur with the above stated views.

Respectfully yours.

Concerned International Citizens

In Discovery Bay, Lan Tau Island, Hong Kong

The People's Republic of China

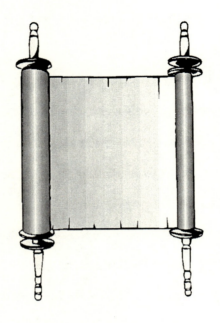

"The Lord preserves the simple: I was brought

low and he helped me.

Return to your rest O my soul, for the Lord

Has dealt bountifully with you."

Psalm116: 6-7

18

Resettling

On September 21, 2002, I returned to my apartment. I immediately re-arranged my bedroom. I hired household helpers to clean and reorder the entire apartment. It was quite a challenge since I was away for almost two years. It was a three-bedroom apartment overlooking the bays on both sides of the high riser. From the large French windows, I could see the far side of Lantau Island. I had an enviable view, compared with some of the exposures of other places where I had lived. Being near the ocean, made the atmosphere in my apartment tranquil and delightful. Living over or by water, is always my most favorite choice of exposure, wherever I may live.

When I left DB to care for my mother, my Chinese land-lord had been simply gracious to allow me to hold on to the apartment for so long by reducing the rent and allowing me to sublet it for only half of the rent. This was a kindness beyond my expectation. As I said in chapter three, he was the best landlord I ever had. Settling in again had some challenges, but I was determined to press on and to be as active as was possible. I wanted to resume living in Discovery Bay in the way I used to before leaving to care for my family.

Extended Absence

I temporarily left DB in January of 2001 to care for my dear mother, in Fort Lauderdale, Florida. First, I had to travel to Jamaica to bring her to America for medical treatment. She literally lived in two worlds. She was a Jamaican, who had permanent residence in the United States where she had studied nursing and worked for many years. At different times in her senior years, she lived with or near me in New York or Fort Lauderdale; however, she would return to her home in Jamaica if I had to travel. She disliked living alone.

The Joys of Living in DB

I liked living in Discovery Bay, (DB) Hong Kong. Like its namesake city – Discovery Bay, Jamaica in the Caribbean, DB is picture perfect with abundant water, majestic hills, and lush greenery and fragrant flowers. I "discovered" this miniature paradise in 1999 on my journey from China, which I "discovered" in 1995.

Discovery Bay, HK, has low air pollution levels; charming high-rise apartment buildings and town houses; schools, churches, and a compact commercial center. DB, with its effective, environmentally sensitive transportation system, which excludes private automobiles, is home to scores of expatriates from many countries. England, Canada, United States of America, China, Malaysia, France, Scotland, Germany, Indonesia, India, Pakistan, Sra Lanka, Australia, the Philippines, Ghana, Trinidad, Nigeria, Zimbabwe, New Zealand and Jamaica, are just a few.

Many pilots, airline attendants and other aviation personnel live in DB. They have easy access to one of the world's largest airports. This is the most international community of families in which I have had the privilege of living. At the beginning of the millennium folks nicknamed Discovery Bay "Delivery Bay" because of the mini population explosion.

Many families, and even their pets, were expecting offspring. Many children live in DB. Saturdays and Sundays are the best days to see the family gatherings and "parades" in the DB Plaza. DB is an ideal place for families. It was for me a haven to relax, write and work. I lived a tranquil life apart from the hustle and bustle of large cities. I would never have thought DB would become the site of double miracles. It has in a most memorable way!!!

"A Great While Before Dawn" (Mark 1:35)

After returning to DB, I reestablished a routine that began between 4:00am and 5:00am, with prayers, meditation, Bible studies, and journaling followed by a long walk through the different areas of Discovery Bay. Often, I walked along the beach closer to the pier for the Catamarans, which took passengers to and from Discovery Bay to Hong Kong Island and Mui Wo. At other times I walked through Peninsula Village up into the hills lined with all kinds of vegetation, noticeably banana plants. Some subsistence gardens had corn, okra, cabbage, sweet potato and string beans.

I was both amazed and thrilled to see the bitter herb *Cerassee*, which is popular in Jamaica and in other Caribbean islands. I also saw it growing wild on fences in Thailand. Here in Discovery Bay, it was growing in one of the small gardens. I searched for the cultivator, who was Filipina. I asked where she got the herb. She said she got it from the Philippines. She gave me a plant of *Cerassee* to add to my window - sill garden. It grew crazily.

I was always intrigued by the wayside "shrines" which graced the path through the hills. They encouraged me to pray in specific ways for truth and clarity. I also prayed for safety when a sign warned me of the presence of alligators, and I saw snakes slithering out of the grass one early morning. I was not frightened. My walk was my daily exercise as well as an extension of my morning prayers. I felt at peace and one with nature as I inhaled the heavenly oxygen-laden air of the mini-forests on both sides of the rocky walk way.

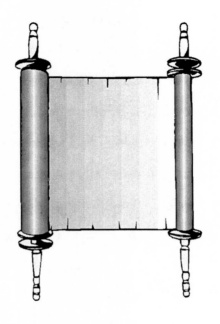

"The cat crossed my path and meowed

loudly as if to say,

"Thank You. I owe you one!"

19

Bold Dog - Scared Cat – Singing Walker

Walking inspired me to sing. One morning as I walked and sang, I heard a dog barking at the top of its canine lungs. It sounded fierce. Its victimized audience was a cat. The dog was on a long leash in front of one of the small, dwellings, which dotted the village and the hillside. Apparently, the cat wanted to share the territory or to pass, but the dog would not let it. I kept singing.

When I got closer to the animals, the dog turned away from the cat, looked at me, sat, and tilted its head as if listening. I changed my song. It kept sitting. It was now my captive audience. The cat got away. I was amused and pleased. I laughed at the strange turn of events for the three of us. I, the singing walker, was in concert with a bold, mesmerized dog, and the scared cat roamed freely. I left the dog sitting and continued on my walk. The cat crossed my path and meowed loudly as if to say, "Thank You. I owe you one!"

I smiled and said, "You are welcome!"

On the way back from my walk, I sang again. There was no raucous this time between the dog and the cat. I heard only the sounds of wild life I could not identify and the splash of waves crashing on the rocks along the beach below the path. As I got closer to the dog, he turned and looked at me.

I started singing. The dog sat for an encore concert. I sang "Elide Weiss", "Oh What a Beautiful Morning" and "Bingo". The dog wagged his tail either in appreciation, disgust or boredom. I forgot how to interpret dog- tail wagging. I thanked it for not barking at me or at the cat at this time. I left it sitting in canine wonderment.

My walks were invigorating, cleansing and loudly expressive. I sang, shouted, screamed, howled, prayed, praised, agonized and cried.

Sometimes I walked uphill to a monastery. This is a contemplative environment. The peace and quiet was almost quantitative. It "touched" me and I "embraced" it. I often sat in the chapel and meditated, prayed and read. I felt settled and free.

My feeling of well being lasted eight weeks. I was well, strong, cheerful, active and productive. I had put behind me the collapse on September 19, 2002 and concentrated on living well.

Incubation

During the sixty-nine days death free period, although I was active, joyful and well, it felt as if I were incubating a "cockatrice's" egg, which would hatch a monstrous creature. I knew something was wrong, but I could not identify it. I just knew that although I felt fine, energetic and alive, there was a heavy foreboding of something hanging over me. I refused to let the spirit of impending doom cripple me. I kept busy, involved and expectant of positive happenings.

A series of small miracles and other pleasantries took place. Some unpleasantries also happened. Surely, both the pleasant and unpleasant were part of Father's flawless orchestration of my affairs.

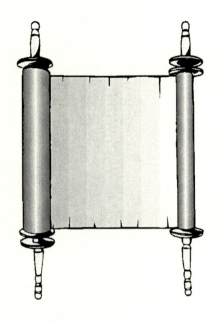

"I even donned my Jamaican National Costume

and created a Jamaican

"Linstead Market" scene selling fruits vegetables

and ackee".

20

Finding The Director

The Switch Bore Fruit

Something pleasant happened when I switched from my usual place of worship to another. It is immaterial at this point what caused the switch. The circumstances leading up to the need to change my church denomination were totally out of everyone's control. It seemed inevitable and took place spontaneously without much fore thought. This, too, was a part of the pre- ordering of my steps.

For three years I had searched for one of the directors of an important organization in Hong Kong. I made numerous phone calls and wrote many letters, yet my efforts were in vain. At the end of the 1999-2000 school year, it became quite urgent to speak with her about a group of Chinese children with whom I had been working. I kept trying, but I was still unable to contact her.

Imagine This!!!

In December 2000, I visited my mother in Jamaica. While there, I attended a Sunday gathering at one of the neighborhood churches. When they recognized visitors, I told them I lived in Discovery Bay, Hong Kong. Immediately, they associated it with Jamaica's North Coast Discovery Bay. At the end of the gathering, they invited visitors to have refreshments. They asked everyone to participate in a bake sale to benefit missions. While mingling with groups of people, a Chinese couple asked if I knew the director of the important organization in Hong Kong.

I was amazed! Over ten thousand miles away from Hong Kong, two people in Jamaica knew the person for whom I had searched in Hong Kong for years. Unimaginable!

I learned for the first time she was "JBC: Jamaican Born Chinese" and had been living and working in Hong Kong for more than thirty years. The couple thought they knew where she was and gave me her phone number.

They also gave me a request for her to help them trace their Chinese ancestry. They were also "JBC", but their parents came from Mainland China and Hong Kong. My search for the director intensified. When I returned to Hong Kong in 2000, I resumed calling her office. I got the same results as before. I could not contact her. Just two weeks after I started attending the DB Anglican Church, "Joy", one of the Chinese members, asked me if I knew the director. She called her name.

Before answering I asked her excitedly,

"Do you know her?"

"Yes. She is my friend." I was both shocked and pleased.

"I am looking for her. I have been searching for her for three years!"

"Well search no more. Please give me your number, and I will have her call you."

I was so joyful! I believe I hugged Joy. I certainly thanked her profusely. At last, both the JBC couple in Jamaica and I have some hope of finding the director. The switch from one congregation to another bore the fruit of finding the director. Amazing grace!

The Director called me the next day, and we made arrangements to meet at my place. I invited two Australian born Chinese to meet her. The first attempt failed. We tried again and met as we had planned. The meeting was wonderful. We laughed, chatted, reminisced about Jamaican life, Australian and Chinese customs. We ate like "little pigs." I even donned my Jamaican national costume and created a Jamaican "Linstead Market" scene "selling" fruits and vegetables and ackee. The fruits and vegetables were real.

The ackee was imaginary in this setting, but it is important to us since it is the chief ingredient in Jamaica's National Cuisine of Ackee and Cod Fish. The Cod Fish, I heard, is from New Foundland, Canada. This is irony at its best.

The ackee is quite interesting. The pod is red and bell-shaped. It opens when it ripens. Each peg looks like a person with a smooth black head without facial features in a pastel yellow jacket with a red vest. When cooked it looks like scrambled eggs. When added to seasoned, fresh or salted codfish, it is absolutely delicious. (See A Word about Ackee at the end)

We added dialog, song, drama, basket balancing act and movement. Life was excellent. I was ecstatic over finding the director and enjoying extreme levity as well as serious intellectual discussions in her home and mine. We spent much time catching up on decades of Jamaican history including some of the current unfavorable conditions of lower educational standards and the exponential increase in crimes.

We spoke extensively about the real reason I searched for her. I told her of the eighteen children I taught and their interest in biblical issues. The director, who had by this time retired from her key position, but was working on special projects within the organization, gave me valuable instructions within the framework of Chinese culture.

The lessons were necessary eye openers. She added important strategies to employ when speaking with Chinese about eternal issues. On one hand, she sounded like a college professor in an advanced class art of communicating with children. On the other hand, she was "down to earth", jolly and friendly. Finding the director was worth the extensive search and three years wait.

The Widening Circle

My circle of friends widened the first day we met the director. Two of my friends and I became the director's friends and she became ours. Despite the fact we were meeting the director for the first time, we felt we were already seasoned friends with her. The camaraderie was natural and fluid. The director embodied the best balance of communication skills and levity.

The following week, we met at the director's home for lunch. I had previously attended luncheons in Chinese home; however, having lunch with the director was unique. She combined Chinese and Jamaican and traditional cuisine and came up with a delicious queenly feast. We did not eat like "little pigs, as we had done at my place.

We dined like royalty with proper etiquette. The director added another dimension by inviting her roommate to display her art collection, so for a while, after lunch, we enjoyed an "impromptu" art gallery presentation.

It was wonderful. We still had a relaxing time of laughter, joking and "labrishing": a Jamaican Patios concept birthed by the indomitable Jamaican Comedienne and Poet Laureate Louise Bennett-Coverley. The circle widened again as two of her friends were added to my circle of friends. I thoroughly enjoyed the dynamic interactions between all the women. The emotions were mostly unpretentious, raw and spontaneous. This made real fun and the creation of lasting friendships possible.

Later, while in the hospital to correct the second ruptured brain aneurysm, the director visited me and told me she, too was a survivor of brain aneurysm. I was encouraged by her miracle and, I felt blessed that some of my friends, my daughters and I had met her.

She wrote in my Red Book:

"God's ways are always best no matter if He has put you on hold. Hang in there. I have been there and survived. Blessings (Psalm32:8)

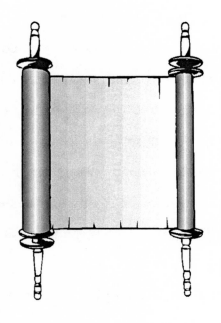

"Set me free from prison

That I may praise your name

Then the righteous will gather about me

Because of your goodness to me".

Psalm 142:7

21

Rare Find: A Jam-African?

❦

When I lived in Jamaica, I joined my church's prison ministry. Since I was completing a spiritual circle, it seemed inevitable I should become an active participant in another prison ministry. During my "Sixty-nine day death-free period", I found someone else when I became involved in the DB Anglican Church's Prison Ministry. The first Sunday I visited a prison in Hong Kong, the ministry coordinator told me of "Ethan Willard", a man he believed to be Jamaican, who was serving a twenty-four year sentence. He did not divulge the reason for such a lengthy sentence. I did not ask for, nor did I assume the reason for his lengthy incarceration.

Ethan was no longer in the prison we visited because he was transferred to a minimum-security facility. I thought that was a favorable step. The coordinator gave me some basic information about him. I kept his address and wrote to him from America almost a year after my visit to the prison and after my second miracle.

I wrote to Ethan in November 2003, so my letter included talk about sorrel, plumb pudding and all the delicious food Jamaicans usually prepare for the Christmas Holidays. I wrote about the customary holiday events beginning with "Grand Market" on Christmas Eve. I reminded him of how we usually stay up all night on Christmas Eve and went to church services as early as 5:00 a.m. on Christmas morning.

After attending the service we would go home, have a special breakfast of ackee and codfish with bammy, dumplings, boiled green bananas and avocado. Real hot cocoa and Blue Mountain coffee would be the hot beverage. Sorrel and ginger beer and rum punch would be the cold drinks throughout the day.

After breakfast, we would sleep if we did not do so in the early morning church service. Later, we would visit friends and relatives then end the solemn day with a huge dinner or two. The next day, December 26, the traditional "Boxing Day", is the time for opening Christmas presents and getting rid of the boxes. It was also the day for garden parties, John Canoe Parades, dances and all kinds of festivities. I thought reminding him of these Jamaican Christmas traditions would make him smile and make his imprisonment for another Christmas more bearable.

He was particularly grateful for my letter since he got it close to Christmas. He replied within a couple of months. Parts of his letter are printed here with his permission:

12 Jan. 2004

Dear Marle,

Top of the morning to you!

Thanks a million for your letter of Nov. 2003, which I got in mid December. Hopefully all is well with you out there. The same can't be said of me in here. I mean life in the slammer can't be fun in any way. Can it? That said though, I thank God I'm in fine health and shape.

I was a bit surprised when I got your letter until I read through it. I guess Rev. Terrence must've furnished you with my personal data. I remembered him commenting casually once that there was a Jamaican working with them in the church, but that was about it then. It's really good of you to write.

I can't tell you enough how glad I'm hearing from you. It's a big morale boost for me knowing that there are people like you out there who care for people like me in the can. You know, it's not uncommon that when one is a situation such as mine sometimes care is hard to come by.

Please forgive me for replying this late. I would've penned you back the moment I got your letter. It's just that December is always a low month for me if you catch what I mean. Since I got stuck here, Dec. has always been a month of reflections for me; it is a time when I spend much time to reminisce the life I used to know. I hope you will understand.

I guess Rev. Terrence must've have told you a bit about me, so this short brief is to let you know that I got your letter. But, I promise to give you a full introduction of myself in my next epistle. Just so you know, I am doing time for drug trafficking. Hopefully that won't dampen your willingness to correspond with me… Your Brother Ethan

The reason for Ethan's imprisonment saddened and troubled me; especially that initially I heard he is Jamaican. I felt a kind of sorrow that was beyond disappointment. I felt betrayed by a fellow citizen. I wondered how his parents and his whole family were feeling, and how terrible it must be for him to be locked away in a foreign prison for twenty – four years. I wondered about his age and why Reverend Terrence told me about him and not about other prisoners. I wondered for a long time, but I did not respond to his letter.

I tried to read between the lines of his letter to get a glimpse of the kind of person he is and what could have made him get involved with illicit drugs. He promised to give me a full introduction of himself in his next "epistle", but I was not sure I wanted to hear from him again. In another part of his letter, he said he would have sent me a snapshot of himself, but he decided against it because he was not sure if it would "go down well" with me. I thought it would have helped me to see what he looked like, but it would not have revealed his character.

I kept his letter safely stashed away. I thought of and prayed for him often, but I did not reply until a year later. I could not pinpoint my reasons for the lengthy delay. I wrote to him, finally. When he responded, he expressed joy at hearing from me again. I was also joyful hearing from him again.

He said he is not Jamaican, but he loves Jamaica. He was mistaken for one because he sang Bob Marley's Reggae, and he has an accent. He is African. I was slightly relieved he was not my countryman, but I still felt sad about the reason for the lengthy imprisonment and the devastating effects it must be having on him, his family and friends.

He was concerned my year's delay in responding to his first letter was because of his drug related crime. After he read my letter, he realized I did not condemn nor condone his actions. I am more concerned about his spiritual, emotional and physical well - being and the valuable lessons he must learn from his experience than I am about his crime.

We still communicate. Through his letters, I learned of his excellent family background and his close relationship with his parents and siblings. He told me of his struggles to start his own small business in 1991 in his native land. He described the unfavorable political, social and economic conditions existing in his country at that time. He told me of his decision to accept a job as a courier for an unknown drug trafficker to raise funds for his failed business. That cost him his freedom. Wisely, he did not blame anyone or any circumstance for his actions. He bore full responsibility, the shame, the remorse and the costly consequence of a twenty-four year prison sentence for a drug law violation in a foreign country.

As his lengthy sentence draws to an end, I lend an ear and a hand to ensure his effective transition back to society instead of deportation to his country. I welcome the opportunity to correspond with him and encourage him in his Christian faith. This experience has strengthened my faith and has taught me many important lessons about our world. Through research on his behalf, I learned many new concepts. I learned about the roles many national governments play directly and indirectly in creating or exacerbating human sufferings and the minimal and often late relief they offer. *I learned about the indomitable spirit of survival in all of us. I saw the need for all of us to be "keepers" of each other.*

I doubt these "by-products" would have resulted if I had not suffered the first ruptured brain aneurysm and fainted in Jacinth's home on September 19, 2002. I would not have met Ethan if her husband, Coleman had not introduced me to the Church's prison ministry. This was by far the most significant event that took place during the incubation and sixty-nine - day-death- free periods of my life in Discovery Bay, Hong Kong. Ethan's story is still unfolding. It is a part of the tapestry of my double miracles.

At the time of completing this book, groups of advocates in New Jersey, New York, Washington D.C., Fort Lauderdale, Florida, Hong Kong, Kingston, Jamaica, Calgary, Alberta, Canada, Dalian, China and Dan Dong, China are involved in peace, justice and human rights advocacy on his behalf. Two American advocates visited him in prison in Hong Kong, in April 2007.

They were impressed by his healthy appearance and calm affect. He is highly respected by the prison administration. The lengthy twenty-four year sentence was reduced to sixteen years and eighteen days because of administrative considerations for exemplary conduct and "above satisfactory" rehabilitation; however, he still faces deportation to Africa. This could be injurious to his health and life

He has challenged the deportation order against him to his country, on the grounds he fears for his life since he would face an uncertain future of re-imprisonment and torture. Two American advocates, with his permission, hand delivered a petition, signed by members of the international community, to the Hong Kong Immigration Department. They also sent petitions to other branches of the Hong Kong government on his behalf in April 2007.

He was released from prison in December 2007. The Hong Kong Immigration Department has decided not to deport him, while they process his "Torture claim" under the United Nations Convention Against Torture and Other Cruel, Inhuman or Degrading Treatment or Punishment (UNCAT). They are holding him in an immigration detention center. If he is able to "establish" this claim, they will not deport him and will consider sending him to a third country, where he will not be tortured. He cannot obtain asylum in Hong Kong. He may obtain a temporary stay to complete travel plans if he is granted the freedom to migrate to a "Safe country" since he has a guarantor.

Recently, several of his advocates went on a "Fact Finding Mission" to Calgary, Alberta Canada, on his behalf. We found several churches, civil and social organizations are empathetic toward him and are poised to welcome him if the United Nations High Commission for Refugees (UNHCR) grants him asylum in Calgary. Some groups wrote letters to the Hong Kong government advocating his freedom after he has been imprisoned for over sixteen years. Other groups sent welcome letters directly to Ethan.

All his advocates wish him the best the Hong Kong Immigration and United Nations High Commissioner for Refugees have to offer. We pray he will succeed in finding "A Safe Country", where he will live the rest of his life in gainful employment. *He will seek for opportunities to work in drug abuse prevention among youthful populations and to advocate on behalf of prisoners in foreign prisons as he pledged.* We believe he has much to offer, and would be an asset instead of a liability to any country that grants him asylum.

This story, which could fill a dozen books, is a part of the miraculous happenings during the death –free and "extreme-make – over" periods of my life in Discovery Bay, Hong Kong. I will forever cherish meeting Ethan through letters and in person. I will also cherish communicating with members of his family.

Above all, I will eternally value the opportunities other ambassadors of good will and I had to join the Master in His work:

"...To bind up the broken hearted; to proclaim

freedom for the captives and release from dark-

ness for the prisoners; to proclaim the year of the

Lord's favor and the day of vengeance of our God;

to comfort all who mourn; and provide for those

who grieve in Zion- to bestow on them a crown of

beauty instead of ashes; the oil of gladness instead

of mourning and a garment of praise instead of a

spirit of despair. They will be called oaks of righ-

teousness; a planting of the Lord for the display of

his splendor. Isaiah 61:1-3 (NIV)

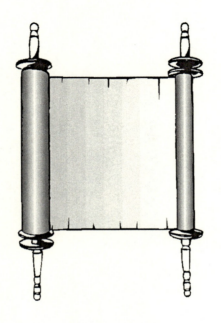

"Yes, even though I walk through the valley

of the shadow of death, I will fear no evil

For You are with me

Your rod and staff

They comfort me".

Psalm 23:4 NIV

22

Before The Second Miracle

My plan was to fly to Dan Dong, China on December 22 to visit special friends for Christmas. Everything was set. I would pick up my ticket early and pack for a white Christmas in China.

I planned to relax for the weekend and then travel several miles from my home in Discovery Bay, Lan Tau Island to the university on the Hong Kong island on the following Monday to complete paper work for future employment.

THE DEFIANT BULLY

On the first day of my weekend, I awoke with a strange headache. Despite the pain, I went for my customary long, power-prayer walk early. I did my biblical studies, prayer, meditation and journaling. On the second day of my weekend I awoke with more of the same unbelievable painful headache. Usually, when I felt a headache coming on, I would speak to it and it would vanish, or I would get relief by doing breathing exercises. At other times, I would simply drink hot water or take a power nap. This time, my success rate was zero percent for two days.

I kept saying, "Go away headache, I have no time for you." It did not budge. Instead, it stood with arms folded; feet firmly planted on the ground, like a defiant bully. It menaced me into Sunday. Each day the headache returned with a vengeance. I took painkillers. Nothing changed. I drank hot water and hot tea; I massaged my temples, neck and fore head. I slept.

When I awoke, the pain grew and escalated from bad to worse and rapidly climbed to worst. Nothing I tried relieved the agony. When it reached the superlative degree of intensity, I knew I was having something worse than the birthing pains I experienced, when I delivered my three children. What was I having? I had no clue.

The Voices

I lived over the bay, so I could hear many sounds. I heard the crashing of waves against the rocks. I knew when a boat was docking or leaving from the churning of the water and the voices of the crew. At nightfall, I heard the crickets creaking, and at daybreak, I heard the birds chirping their wake - up calls. I heard a fascinating sound like a cow mooing right by the shore. Later, I learned it was a kind of toad or frog in the marsh on the far side of the pier.

Some of the sounds in my apartment were not fascinating. They were threatening and eerie. I was not sure who or what made them or if they were just voices in my head. Several times, I heard a menacing taunt, **"You gonna die!"** At first I just listened to the soothsayer and prayed. The taunting stopped for a while, but as it neared the sixty-ninth day after the first miracle of surviving a near - death experience, it started again. The frequency of the taunts increased on November 22, 2002, when my headache started and over the two days following as my headache worsened. I decided since I was the only rent-paying occupant of my apartment, I would let nothing or no one, real or imagined, drive me out or drive me crazy.

I prayed for direction and focus. I had learned not to pray for patience or peace. I was given peace. I must cultivate patience. I was directed to several scriptures. The first is from *John 14:27 "Peace I leave with you; my peace I give unto you: not as the world gives, I give unto you. Let not your heart be troubled, neither let it be afraid."* Oh what comfort!

The direction was for me to take the legacy of peace that I have and apply it to my current situation. How would I do that? I recalled songs about peace and sang them. I recalled more scriptures about peace and repeated them. I internalized the truths about the author of my peace (Eph 2:14). What about the thoughts of loosing my mind? That need was already provided for in the scriptures in *II Timothy1: 7, Paul declares, "For God has not given us the spirit of fear, but of power and of love and of a sound mind."* Applying this declaration to my painful situation then, empowered me to: "Let patience have her perfect work…" (James 1:3) I needed to wait and see the kind of "egg I was incubating."

DEATH ON THE HORIZON

On Saturday, November 23, 2002, the menacing taunt came again.

"You gonna die! You gonna die!"

I did not stop my ears this time. First, I laughed. Then I raised my head, squared my shoulders, pushed out my chest and lifted my hands like a sergeant giving a command and shouted the word from Psalm 118:17, *"I shall not die, but live and declare the works of the Lord!"*

"Did this stop the taunt?" "Yes, it did".

I did not let my guard down though. I continued to pray and to trust for a clear indication of why I was having such a hellacious headache? Why was a heavy foreboding hanging over me?

Suddenly, I remembered what Jakes, who saw me after I was escorted back to my apartment on the day I fainted, told me.

"I saw death printed all over your face. Your eyes rolled over, and your face was pale." I listened to him then in astonishment. I now connected what he said with the taunting voices. I thought, **"So, it is true I may die soon."** I felt the incubation period was ending.

THE EGG WAS ABOUT TO HATCH.

I believe the "egg" I had been incubating for sixty-nine days was about to hatch its dreadful monster. I was not afraid. I had learned through life experience and the scriptures: death is an ever-present reality. **I was prepared, but I was not ready to die.** I believe I have more important work to do. When the egg hatches, I would face whatever emerges with all the faith and courage I have. I would focus on the positive and let nothing intimidate or frustrate me. **My master always has a better plan.**

SEALED

I realized something else. There was another presence and voice in my apartment. On November 22, 2992, the first day of the hellacious headaches, I was sitting in my living room trying to read and write despite the severe pain. I distinctly heard another voice – calm, reassuring and nurturing. The quiet voice seemed to speak from within me. Perhaps it was my self-preserving inner voice.

"Come away. Leave what you are doing and go kneel by the foot of your bed, so I may bless you."

The direction was precise. I rose from my chair. I walked into my bedroom. I knelt at the foot of my bed with my face toward the window. I closed my eyes. The gentle voice continued.

"Be still. Pray not. Talk not. Sing not. Be still. I will bless you."

I surrendered completely to the promptings of the gentle voice. I closed my eyes and waited for more directions. There was none. Instead, there was a deep settling feeling within me. I felt as if someone was pouring a cool substance on me from my head. It flowed all over me down to the tips of my toes and surrounded me as I knelt. I felt enclosed as if I were sealed and isolated from my surroundings, yet I felt free. Soon, I felt warm and light as if a burden was lifted from my shoulders.

I kept kneeling, and it seemed I had fallen asleep. When I awoke, the atmosphere in my apartment felt different. There was a refreshing breeze coming off the water through the open windows. There was a serene quietness in the atmosphere. Whatever strange thing was happening seemed to be ending, but I was being protected from its effects. Despite the severity of the headache, I felt well and calm.

"...A FRIEND IN DEED"

Later my friend Carrie came to see me. When I opened the door for her, the glare from the bright hallway lights made me squint. She knew I had been having a severe headache. When she saw me squinting and holding my head, she told me I was having a migraine. Her visit was brief. When she left, I wondered what could be causing the violent headache. I decided I would go to the doctor on Monday, two days away.

The next day, Sunday, our congregation was having a Thanksgiving Feast for which members were encouraged to bring a favorite covered dish. I made sweet potatoes with raisins, pineapple, cinnamon and nutmeg. I topped it with brown sugar and melted butter. **"Yummy!"** What used to be the easiest dish for me to make became a difficult task. I had to stop often to regain my strength. Coping with the severe headache had sapped my energy. I hoped to attend the service and take the dish with me. I retired early and had a peaceful rest despite the torturous headache.

Sunday, November 24, 2002 arrived, so did another intense bout of headache. I felt as if all the drums of the world were resounding in my head. The vibration weakened me. In addition, my eyes became sensitive to light. The dimmest ray of light made it impossible for me to open my eyes. I called Carrie and asked her to take my dish to the church. I was too ill to attend the service and luncheon. When she arrived, she once again stated I was having a migraine and encouraged me to take it easy and to rest.

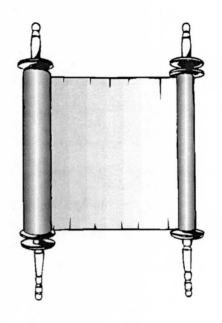

"My grace is sufficient for you, for my strength is

Made perfect in weakness

More gladly therefore will I rather glory in my

infirmities,

that the power of Christ may rest upon me

II Corinthians 12: 9"

23

My Head! My Head!

I followed Carrie's advice. I remained in bed practically all morning. I rose only when it was absolutely necessary. With my plan to visit my doctor the next day, I tried to cope as best as I could. I ran out of painkillers, so I drank teas, hot water, Chinese bitter melon juice and freshly made fruit juices. For two days, I did not walk after my early morning prayers and meditation. My headache continued to be hellacious. It was too severe. Numberless times, all I could do was to hold my head and say, **"My head, my head"** like the young boy in the **double miracle** story in II Kings 4:19 KJV.

He was the product of a miracle through the prophet Elisha because his parents had not been able to have a child. He was really a reward to them for their kindness to the prophet. They had entertained the prophet Elisha and his servant Gehazi with meals frequently. Later, the Shunammite woman persuaded her husband to build a "little chamber on the wall and furnished it with a bed, a table and a candlestick" for Elisha. The prophet expressed his gratitude by praying for a child for the childless couple.

One day the boy was with his father in the field when he suddenly said to him, **"My head! My head!"** His father took him to his mother, who kept him on her lap until he died at noon.

My conjecture is this young boy, too, must have had the "worst headache of his life". My guess is he died from a ruptured brain aneurysm or some form of cerebral hemorrhage.

Later through another miracle, the boy's life was restored after his mother forcefully confronted Elisha about giving them a child when they had not asked for one. This was a double miracle.

MY SOLILOQUY

This story, and the voices I had been hearing, seemed to indicate something serious was about to happen to me. Like Hamlet, in the Shakespearian play by the same name, I found I was talking out aloud to myself:

"God I realize something is happening in my body. I do not know what, but something is happening. I believe I could easily die in this place, but please do not let it happen. I live alone.

Father, can you imagine what would happen if I were to die here by myself? No one would find me for days! My children would know even later! I would be decomposing! People would be shocked and some would be angry enough to blame you or me. Father, "Let your mercy say no" to my death. "LET YOUR MERCY SAY NO!!!!!!!"

I shouted! I begged! A song came to my mind. I started to sing it. "Mercy said no. I'm not gonna let you go...."

"Oh! I really don't know the words".

I tried to get off the bed. It was taking me longer than usual, but I will make it. There! Finally, I got up! I started talking out aloud again

"Father my head is pounding mercilessly. Please let your mercy say NO! Say no to my death! I plead with you Father. Let me live to declare your works and praise your magnificent name. I started to sing again.

"Mercy Said No. I'm not going to let you die. Mercy said no…"

Father I feel weak I have to lie down again. PLEASE HELP me! Let your mercy say NO!"

I lay on the bed again – listening for voices. I started thinking what my next action should be to get rid of this terrible headache. I assumed my blood pressure was high. Late Sunday afternoon, I thought I would check my blood pressure. I decided to go to DB plaza to purchase a blood pressure monitor. At 4:30pm, I called Watson's for the price and for their closing time. The store was closing at 5:30 p.m.

The walk to the plaza would be only ten minutes. I had enough time.. I got up and slowly got dressed in a jogging suit to cope with the chill. Then I lay on the bed again for fifteen minutes. I got up and decided to leave. I felt weak. I could hardly move, but I made it to the kitchen door. I looked through the glass at the upper part of the door and saw it was 5:00 p.m. on the wall clock.

More Voices

As I placed my hand on the kitchen doorknob, I heard it. A gentle voice clearly said, "Tmay, these are not ordinary headaches. Seek help."

"Okay, I know that!" I would always answer voices.

I walked into the kitchen to get some Chinese bitter-melon juice. I heard it was good for high blood pressure.

Since it was clear now I would not make it to DB Plaza to get the blood pressure monitor, I decided to find relief any way I could. As soon as I finished drinking the bitter melon juice, I heard the gentle voice again. It impressed on me to be quiet again. It seemed very near to me. I stood by the kitchen window looking wistfully toward DB Plaza.

The quiet, sympathetic voice cajoled, "Seek help your headache is not ordinary. Seek help." I had my answer to my unasked question. I needed no more prompting.

I turned slowly to leave the kitchen. *Suddenly, I heard a faint "pop". I felt as if something broke in my head and trickled down inside the right side of my neck. The headache seemed to lessen some, but my neck began to stiffen.*

"This seems serious," I thought. I knew the help I would seek. I prayed for God's help and then walked slowly to the bedroom and sat on the edge of the bed.

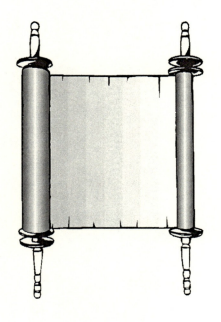

"God is our mighty fortress

Always ready to help in times of trouble

And so, we won't be afraid…"

Psalm 46:1 (The Contemporary English Version)

24

999

The Number That Saved The Day!!!!!!!!

I picked up the telephone and **dialed 999. It was only a week before my headaches started that I learned this is the emergency number for Hong Kong.** When I asked my friend Kim "What is the emergency number for Hong Kong?" She brushed me slightly on the right arm and said, "You don't need the emergency number. You are so fit. You are so healthy."

"Yes, but you never know. I may need it for myself or for someone else."

She reluctantly told me, **"It's 999".**

I repeated: **"999."** I memorized it immediately.

When I called, the response was quick. I asked for ambulance service. The soft-spoken operator wanted to know why. I told her I had been having a severe headache that would not go away, even with painkillers. She asked if anyone would be accompanying me. I told her yes. After hanging up from **999,** I called my friend Carrie, who had told me to call her if I needed help. I was a little hesitant to call since she had houseguests and would have had to leave them. Carrie assured me it was okay. I thanked her for her kindness

I hung up and decided to open the door ahead of the emergency team's arrival. I got up slowly from the bed. As I did, I felt a stabbing pain in the center of my head. My neck stiffened, forcing me to walk straight up like a toy soldier. I walked at a snail pace taking short, stiff, toy – soldier – like – kicks, so my elevated eyes would see where my feet were landing.

As soon as I opened the door and left it ajar, the phone rang. I had to do a toy soldier shuffle, while holding my neck and head lifelessly stiff. I made it to the phone in time. It was Carrie telling me she was on her way.

As soon as I hung up, the emergency team arrived. I was pleased with their prompt arrival, but I felt something was missing. Where were the paramedics with stretcher, a stethoscope to listen to my heart, a thermometer to take my temperature, and a sphygmomanometer to test my blood pressure? There were no vital signs paraphernalia. What they had was a small, red wheelchair, abundant courtesy; impeccable bedside manners and genteel patience. They asked me a few questions about my condition and quickly determined I needed to go to the hospital.

"Where is your friend, who is coming with you?" The question was still on their lips when Carrie arrived. The men exchanged cordial greetings with her. She asked to which hospital, and how they would be taking me. They told her to Princess Margaret Hospital in Kowloon. It was the closest to access by road, by going through the DB tunnel.

This tunnel opened in May 2000 allowing travelers to get to Discovery Bay by buses and to connect with the trains. Prior to the tunnel opening, the only way to travel to and from DB was by ferries.

"Are you not going by ferry?" she asked.

I dreaded the prospect. "Hurry!!!!!" was the word of the moment for me. Going by ferry might have been soothing. Then we would have to be concerned about another transfer by land on one of Hong Kong's busy streets to slow us down. Any bumping up and down might cause my head to explode.

"No," they replied. By road is better and quicker.

"Thank God". I sighed.

"Come," one of the men called. As I got up slowly from the bed, another man assisted me.

"Pack a bag in case they keep me," I said.

Carrie moved around quickly and gathered clothing items from various drawers and closets.

The man assisting me let go of my arm, so I could go slowly into the bathroom to gather toilet articles. I handed my cosmetic case to Carrie, and the man resumed holding my arm.

My neck was stiff and painful. **Because of this, I wondered if I had spinal meningitis, as my youngest child Alaya had at eleven months of age, but I felt safe and peaceful.**

I marveled at the fact that I had slept well for the two nights I had been hurting so dreadfully. My sedative was: **Psalm 4:8**

"I will both lay me down in peace and sleep

For you Lord only make me to dwell in safet*y***".**

After discovering this scriptural "sleeping pill" during less peaceful times, nothing kept me awake. Not even the threat of death disturbed me now.

Who Prepared Me?

When I reached my desk, I remembered my emergency lists.

I said, "Wait," to the man holding my arm and broke free to get the lists.

"Here Carrie", I said.

"What's this?" she asked.

"Emergency contacts."

"When did you write these?"

"Long ago."

"Wow!" Carrie was surprised at my preparedness.

"Please give one to Jacinth, and you keep one." I thought they were incomplete but would suffice.

The emergency crew led me to the door on foot and then put me in the small, red wheel chair for the ride from the fifteenth floor to the ambulance in the courtyard. I was still holding my head stiffly like a toy soldier.

I hoped I was elegant. In emergencies, I am always concerned if I am gracious, decent, and lady-like, and if my clothes, especially my undergarments, were clean and attractive. It was an important part of my Caribbean cultural heritage. When going to the doctor, we took special care of our personal appearance on top and beneath. This time, despite having the worst headaches of my life, was no exception.

When Carrie, the attendants and I got to the ambulance, the men transferred me to a cot in the back of the ambulance and strapped me down. I closed my eyes and started praying silently immediately. I prayed all the way to Princess Margaret Hospital in Kowloon on the large Hong Kong Island. I am not sure how many miles it is from Discovery Bay, where I lived. The traveling time by ambulance was forty minutes.

I tried to remain composed and positive. Since I had no clue what serious thing was happening to me, I kept praying silently to the Father to reveal the cause of my unbearable headache to the doctors at Princess Margaret Hospital. They would tell me what is wrong with me.

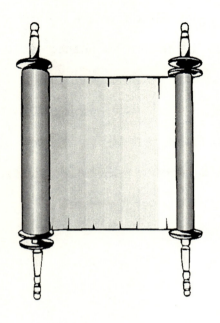

"See; I have refined you though not as silver;

I have tested you in the furnace of affliction.

For my own sake, for my own

name's sake I do this.

How can I let myself be defamed?

I will not yield my glory to another".

Isaiah 48:10-11 NIV

25

Arriving At Princess Margaret Hospital

November 24, 2002: UNFORGETTABLE DAY!

I arrived at Princess Margaret Hospital at about 6:00 p.m. fully conscious and aware. I saw the two ambulance attendants and my friend Carrie. I knew when the gentlemen removed me from the ambulance, put me back in the quaint, red, wheel chair and wheeled me to an elevator. I recalled getting onto the elevator, but I cannot recall getting off. I lost awareness.

There must have been an emergency room where they gave critically ill patients prompt attention. I saw no doctor, nurse or any other hospital personnel or the other patients who might have come in before or after I arrived. I do not recall anyone speaking with me, asking my name and what brought me to the hospital. I do not recall that the doctors told me what was wrong with me, and what they planned to do about it. *All I can recall is being moved through a web of hallways like narrow, dark tunnels. I do not recall who moved me or how and to where.*

The British, Royal Connection

In Discovery Bay, where I lived, there are private doctors' offices but no hospitals, so Princess Margaret in Kowloon was the hospital the emergency crew chose. I felt an affinity to the place just from hearing the name. The hospital was obviously named for the late Princess Margaret of England, the deceased younger sister of Queen Elizabeth, II. Princess Margaret died at age seventy-one on February 9, 2002. Because of Jamaica's relationship with England since the year 1665, I felt we were connected to the royal family. I thought Princess Margaret resembled my precious, first cousin Florence.

Entering a hospital named for the princess, brought back significant childhood memories of the death of her father King George, VI and the coronation of her sister Queen Elizabeth, II.

As part of a musical group of elementary, school children in Jamaica, I had the joyous privilege of singing for the queen and her family at Sabina Park during her coronation tour of the British Commonwealth in 1953. I still remember the silly songs we sang.

Additionally, there is a Princess Margaret Hospital in Jamaica, my homeland. It is located in Morant Bay in the parish of Saint Thomas. Entering Princess Margaret Hospital was like entering familiar waters. I felt protected. Despite this initial safe feeling, I still did not know how protected I was for about nine days between November 24 and December 03, 2002. The reports, verbal and written, stated I was conscious, talkative and sometimes maudlin. No one was sure why I cried. Those, who were with me, observed I wrote mostly everything the doctors and the nurses said. In this way I had some information about my condition and the plan to correct it. Although I have no recollection of speaking with anyone, the pre – surgery notes are in my handwriting.

"IN LA-LA LAND"

I was grateful to have arrived safely at the hospital. At last, I was at a place where they would discover my problems and treat them. It was Sunday, November 24, 2002. I recalled getting out of the ambulance. I saw the friendly faces of the ambulance attendants. I am not sure they call them "Paramedics" in Hong Kong. I saw my friend Carrie on my right holding my belongings. I heard her comforting voice and felt her reassuring pat on my shoulder as she told me I would be okay. I recalled getting onto an elevator.

As soon as the doors closed, all my awareness of everything was closed out, too. After I regained awareness, several times someone asked me if I remembered saying certain things or doing certain things. "Do you remember what the doctor said?" "No". "Do you remember who came to see you?" My answer was always "No!"

Twilight Days

During the first nine days of my thirty-day hospitaliza-tion, although the reports stated I was conscious and appeared alert, I was unaware of most of my actions as well as other people's actions. I was also totally unaware of visitors during the days immediately before and after my surgery.

Several persons, including my pastor's wife, told me they visited me and repeated the gist of our conversations. I had no recollection of their presence and their interactions with me. I wondered how this could have been. I am certain they must have wondered, too.

The most remarkable examples of my amnesia are not having any recollection of writing the poem "Litany of Love" and of writing the medical notes from the surgeons' explana-tion of their findings and the surgery they recommended.

Later, when my daughter Alaya, of whose presence I was not always aware, asked, "Don't you remember writing the poem and explaining "Litany" then reading it to me?" I did not remember. I knew something had been out of my control when I forgot something that significant. I found myself repeating verbatim people's questions or statements and becoming annoyed at my lack of short-term memory. I felt something was missing from my life.

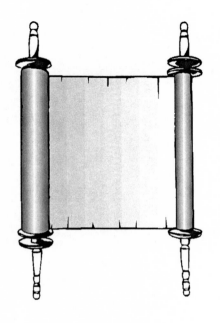

"I was delighted to see I had not lost

knowledge of the happenings

although I still cannot recall

even writing them down".

26

Admitted To Princess Margaret

"Ghost Writer"

Some one, most likely one of the neurosurgeons, must have told me about the plan to operate and why. The notes I found, when I returned to America, confirmed this, yet I have no mental recall of having written them. All about my admission would have been lost if it were not for my habit of writing everything in a book or on scraps of paper. In this instance, I became my own "ghost writer."

My other self, whom I will call **"Topsy"**, was aware, coherent and well. She acted on behalf of my unaware, incoherent self, who was walking in the "valley of the shadow of death." This was *"ghost writing"* in the truest sense of the word.

After returning to the U.S, I went through my belongings and found a sheet of paper. At the top it has Chinese characters, the English alphabet and grids to write in information. Obviously, it was used as an in take sheet for patients admitted to the neurological ward.

My guess is I asked for something on which to write, and someone gave me one of these sheets and a pencil. I was delighted to see I had not lost knowledge of the pre-surgery happenings although I still cannot recall even writing them down. I have no memory of anyone telling me what was wrong with me, nor do I recall what tests they did to find out.

The triage sheet, on which I wrote, holds some of the pieces to the puzzle of my amnesia, but it offers no whole solution. What I wrote appears here unedited. Check the spelling errors. On one side of the paper I wrote:

Diagnosis: suspected ruptured aneurism in (at) the area of the posterior communicating artery. Aramlong-opening of the skull bone. Clipping of aneurism bulge from the wall of an artery. Deposit fats or fungal effect or congenital. A layer thinned vessel wall mostly-of bifuc….X (turning pt. Of 2 arteries caused the flow of blood to rupture.

OT. @ 10:30 (am/pm?)/. Surgery is at……..

Vaso spasm-blood goes out instead of staying in the brain.

Hydrocephaly sis

HDU1691 29901163 GONE TO OPERATION

It is clear someone spoke to me about my condition and told me the outcome of my admission to the hospital would be the clipping of a ruptured brain aneurysm. I wrote this under much stress not fully grasping its seriousness. It is hurried, incomplete and incoherent. Making sense of what I wrote is challenging. This is the extent of the notes I made upon my admission. I still have no idea what some of it mean. I did not record, nor do I recall the questions I must have asked.

The notes were not in logical order. They were scribbled all over the paper as if I were physically twisting and turning.

Making Sense Out of Nonsense

I still do not know what some of my notes mean. The medical persons I asked to help me make sense of them could not tell me what *"Aramlong opening of the bone skull"* means.

I have a faint memory of one of the surgeons telling me, I am unsure when, about boring three holes in my skull and clipping the aneurysm. Could these holes be the "Aramlong opening"? My cousin Jackie, a physical therapist, helped me research surgical openings for craniotomy, but we found nothing.

Trophy of Grace

A year after my surgery, an indentation appeared in the right side of my skull. It seemed one of the holes, which were bored for the surgery, had caved in. It troubled me. I thought my whole skull would cave in, and I would need to have more brain surgery. One neurologist explained that not packing one of the openings after the surgery could have caused part of my skull to cave in. He told me I would have to live with it instead of having risky, expensive reconstructive surgery. I am content to "live with it".

I decided to call it "My Trophy of Grace". This indentation on the right side of my skull will always remind me of when "Mercy said NO!" to my death.

Many people, especially children, ask me, "What's wrong with your head?" I am glad whenever they ask. I cheerfully tell them it is my trophy of grace.

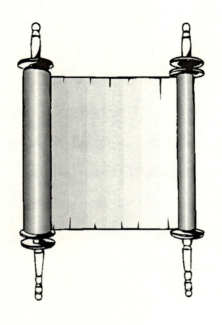

"You satisfy me with your presence

You bring to me

Those you appointed to love me"

27

Litany Of Love

After making these notes, I apparently turned the paper and wrote on the other side this original poem:

<u>Litany of Love</u>

Here I am Lord

From Bed I Block A6

Princess Margaret Hospital, Hong Kong

I am propped up with pillows

And hooked up with Foley Catheter

And all…

With no where to look but up

****

So, I look up to you Father

While I hold the gift

Your gift of another day

Gratefully in my hands

I thank you Life of my life

For your indescribable

Faithfulness to me

****

You are with me

On this new day

As you awaken me from

The oblivion of night

Your mercy preserved me

To find you with me

And I with you

Glorious union of unfading love

My Ishi forever!

****

My husband, lover of my soul

Joy of my heart

My Shepherd who leads me

By the still waters

And the pastures green

And spreads before me

A sumptuous feast

Right before the eyes of my

Enemies

You satisfy me with your presence

You bring to me

Those you appointed to love me

****

I praise you magnificent Father!

You are through Jesus

My wonderful Savior

And my intercessor

You are through Holy Spirit

My Paraclete; my comforter

You, yourself, are my husband

My provider; my healer

****

I praise you and thank you

For all you have done

All you are doing and

All you will do for me

You assure me of:

Your best always

Great is your faithfulness

Thank you. Your Grateful

Daughter Tmay

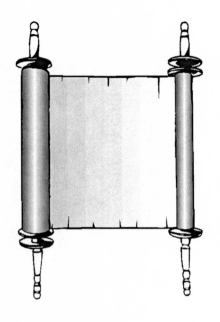

"I hold the splendid daylight in my hands

Inwardly grateful for another day…"

George Campbell

28

The Joy Of Not Knowing

Deathbed Rituals and "Topsy"

The fact I could have written the notes about my diagnosis and the poem while unaware and while having an indescribable headache was *truly miraculous*. Each time I read the notes about my diagnosis and the poem, I realized they were deathbed scenarios. Although I still cannot recall writing them, I believe once the doctors told **"Topsy"** my unaware self about a ruptured brain aneurysm, she must have thought, "Oh boy! This is serious! This is my end"! Then she decided to express her love and gratitude instead of fear for the imminent death and wrote the poem.

Others also thought it was the end for me. I learned later the hospital chaplain gave me pre-surgery rites. The surgeons called my daughters often, and someone from Discovery Bay called my daughter Jessica in Hastings, New York and told her to come quickly since I might not "make it". Even one of the excellent surgeons told me, when he saw my remarkable recovery, that he thought I would not have made it. WOW!

No Profanity

In retrospect, my poem, I believe, was a kind of last rites to myself. Although cursing was never a habit for me, I was glad I did not utter a string of deathbed profanities or expressions of hopelessness as I heard others had done. Instead, it was this poem, which reflects my childhood love of poetry and my close relationship with the Holy One, whom I knew would be with me to the very end in a "Glorious union of unfading love. My Ishi forever!"

Strange Discovery

When I returned to America to be with my daughters for a while, I found the paper on which I had scribbled the diagnostic notes and the poem. I read them both. I thought someone else must have written the notes for me since some words were misspelled. I considered myself an excellent speller. I had not written the word "aneurysm" before, so spelling it a-n-e-u-r-i-s-m demonstrated my ignorance of both the word and the severity of the problem.

Verifying Mysterious Writing

I liked the poem, but I did not think I had written it although I was familiar with the word "Litany". A closer look at the handwriting convinced me I had written the poem. To be sure, I asked my daughter Alaya. "Who wrote the notes and the poem?" She answered swiftly.

"Mom, you wrote them. Don't you remember you asked me before? Do you remember...?"

"Blink!!!!!!!" A signal went off in my head as Alaya spoke. I remembered something. I cut her off.

"Ooops!!!!" I said laughing. Then I asked,

"Did you ask me what is a Litany?"

"I believe I did." She spoke firmly.

I had a long – term flash back to my memory of my Calabar Primary School days in Jamaica when I had memorized "Litany" by George Campbell (1945).

"Yes, I remember I told you I got the idea from George Campbell who wrote `Litany` in

A Treasury of Jamaican Poetry, and I recited a few lines:

"I hold the splendid day light in my hands.

Inwardly grateful for another day

Thank you life.

Day light like a fine fan spread from my hand.

Day light like Scarlet Poinsettia...

Day light like sea sparkling

With white horses...." (Foaming waves)

Alaya admitted, "Yes, I remember you telling me of some guy who wrote a litany."

"I still don't remember writing it, nor do I recall you reading it."

"Don't worry. It will all come back." She assured me.

She seemed certain I would regain my memory. I thought, "Man, this is so strange! I recalled a poem from my elementary school days almost a century ago, but I cannot remember most of my sensory activities only a few days or a few hours old. How could I have been so totally unaware of my actions and still survived two, ruptured brain aneurysms?"

Protective Wisdom

After some deep thinking, I concluded my lack of awareness was perhaps partly the reason I survived. I was removed from the equation, at least temporarily, so especially qualified people could handle my special and critical needs without any interference, direction or objection from me. This is protective wisdom. I call it the miracle of not knowing.

I had to ask various people to help me fill in the missing pieces. Carrie told me that on the day I was admitted, I "vomited buckets", and I kept asking for more pillows under my head to ease the headache. I guess those were the pillows, which propped me in my poem "Litany of Love". I do not recall them, nor do I recall regurgitating "buckets" as Carrie told me.

I **PASSSIONATELY** dislike vomiting. I would usually remember the wrenching, churning, squeezing, gasping actions of my stomach and the pool of slimy, disgusting, variegated stuff I regurgitated for a long time! This time I did not. I just heard and read about it. **Thank goodness!**

Long Term/ Short Term

Preparing some one for Craniotomy is vastly different from preparing one for Appendectomy. Although there is always a sense of urgency related to any surgery, operating on the brain is often thought of as having greater risks than operating to remove an appendix from the large intestines. I remember my appendectomy of 1973 in St. Andrew's Hospital in Jamaica and all the conditions before and after the surgery as if it had happened recently.

I recall none of the diagnostic procedures, which preceded the surgery, nor do I recall the postoperative conditions immediately following my brain surgery in Princess Hospital in Hong Kong in 2002. The actual surgery would probably be unknown to me since I would have been heavily anesthetized for the "cracking" of my skull, but I should have remembered something about what preceded and followed the surgery.

Many days after I had brain surgery, I met members of the Pastoral Team. Two of the chaplains told me they had come to see me and prayed with me before I had my surgery. I cannot believe I missed this opportunity to talk with fellow chaplains and to fellowship with them as they ministered to me.

The troubling thing is they might have thought I was aware of their presence when we first met and later thought it strange I did not recognize them. I became annoyed with myself for dwelling in the "La-la-land" of intermittent unawareness and appearing so foolish to others and myself. I decided to fix this troubling situation by writing daily.

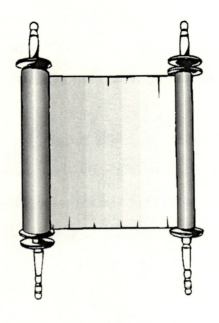

"I could record notes, which would help me keep
track of my remaining days in the hospital
and solve the mystery of the missing pieces".

29

The Red Book

I am not sure how I got a red book, nor does anyone else know. I might have asked for a book, but I do not remember. The book is a red, twin-wire hard cover "Boston notebook." The idea was to have a book in which my visitors would record their names and anything they wished to write. I could record notes, which would help me keep track of my remaining days in the hospital and solve the mystery of the missing pieces.

In the inside cover, on the gray pages, are these words, "Visitors and friends Log: Tmay's remarkable hospitalization and miraculous recovery after a masterful brain surgery at the great Princess Margaret Hospital, Kowloon,

Hong Kong; November 24 – December 2002.

Praise God!"

On the first white page there is this note, from my daughters.

"To: Friends of Tmay. Thank you so much for your visit. Please turn the page and kindly leave your name address, phone number, email and a brief message to Tmay. Thank you!"

These words were written below, on the same page in prose-poetry style with green ink in what appears to be in my handwriting:

"To: All who visit me in PMH

God bless you for taking the time to come and visit me.

You might have brought a card.

You might have brought a gift. You might have brought some lovely flowers

To be sure, everyone brought something.

A smile on your lovely face

A prayer on your grateful lips

A thought on your peaceful mind

A wish from deep in your heart

Are some of God's rarest treasures

And each of you brought these and more

Your hugs, your kisses, your winks

Your wishes for good health

Messages from others, your jokes

Your rocky-like sweets, your laughter

All bring me a taste of heaven here on earth.

God bless you for caring

May He reward you always with the manifested presence of Himself.

Tmay 12/12/02

I was amazed at how many persons, including doctors and nurses, took the time to write their thoughts in my red book. In addition to helping me to be aware of some of the people who visited me, they provided me with their contact information for the future. Having the red book also encouraged me to write my thoughts. Writing was therapeutic for me. The self- therapy has been an effective part of my rapid recovery. My ability to spell gradually improved. My short-term memory also improved.

The entri.es in the my red book will be a major part of:

FOR YOUR JOURNEY, Volume II Double Miracles in Discovery Bay, Hong Kong.

I quote one entry to give a taste of some of the sentiments my visitors expressed:

PMH

12-12-02, 2:40pm.

Dear Tmay,

Glad to see you happy and smiling a lot more. Back to your old tricks again – joking, clowning around and bringing laughter to those with whom you come in contact. You have been a blessing to many in the past. May God continue to guide you in the many surprises of life...Ps.40: 12. Wishing you a speedy recovery and a pleasant trip home to the

States to be with family. Keep in touch. Lots of love…

A friend.

The many entries in the red book are truly inspiring to me. They are reminders of life even in the "shadow of the valley of death". I am eternally grateful to all who took the time to express their thoughts. They have given me much to aid me on my journey to full recovery.

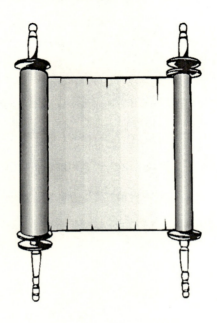

"We are concerned about our daughters.

We hope they will learn from their grandmother

and from us and become

educated about this "silent killer.

If they are vigilant of they health and attuned to

their bodies, they, too,

will survive brain aneurysms.

They might be able to escape having any. This is

my prayer".

30

Becoming Aware

I entered the hospital on November 24, 2002. I had surgery the same day, to correct a ruptured aneurysm. According to both unofficial and official reports, I did not lose consciousness. I was able to talk, respond to questions, and even initiate conversations.

The big problem is I cannot recall much of anything, which occurred just before my surgery. I do not recall seeing or speaking with doctors or even Carrie, "my guardian angel", who accompanied me to Princess Margaret Hospital.

Some one had to admit me; however, I do not recall the triage process at all. My guardian angels, Carrie and Jacinth,

Jenna and other people who saw me during the early days of my hospitalization filled in some of the missing pieces of the puzzle for me. I still think there is much I will not know about what happened when I had the first rupture while I was in Discovery Bay. I also will not know what occurred during the first nine days after I had the second rupture and the brain surgery.

MEDICAL DIAGNOSIS:

Although I had written the notes of the surgeons' diagnosis of my condition and their plan to operate, I had "amnesia for the event". Several days after the surgery, I was coherent enough to hear from both surgeons and to understand what was the urgency and gravity of my condition. I also learned many new medical terms.

The diagnosis was: "Ruptured cerebral aneurysm" The rupture occurred in the Posterior Communicating Artery (PcomA).

Questions About Cerebral Aneurysms:

Since I did not know about aneurysms and what would have caused an artery to rupture in my brain, I asked a flurry of questions: "What is an aneurysm? Where is it detected? How is it detected? What are the symptoms? Can one treat an aneurysm before it ruptures? What happens when an aneurysm ruptures? Why did I have ruptured brain aneurysms? Is brain aneurysm hereditary?

I consciously asked these questions several days after my brain surgery when my amnesia was ending, and I was becoming more aware of my environment. I did not recall asking similar questions when I was admitted to Princess Margaret Hospital until I found the paper on which I had scribbled the notes and the poem among my belongings. My notes showed I had asked some questions for which I got responses.

Some Answers

Aneurysm: An aneurysm is a "retrograde bleed or blood clot". The blood in the artery "bunches up". The pressure causes the artery to rupture and the blood to flow out of the artery instead of flowing through it. *Essentially, this is an aneurysm.*

What are the causes of cerebral aneurysms?

The doctors said the causes of an aneurysm vary from person to person, but they may include fatty deposits, parasites, a weakness in an artery, uncontrolled hypertension, smoking and congenital factors. My surgeons were not sure what caused mine.

Some Symptoms

These, like the causes of aneurysms,

may differ from person to person.

Severe headache, sensitivity to light and noises and hearing voices were the three major symptoms of which I was aware in my case. I did not vomit until I got to the hospital, and I was totally unaware of this. The surgeons told me I had what they call "the worst headache" in the medical arena.

This was definitely an understatement for me. I estimated my headache to be triply worse than the one I had when a rock busted my forehead, while I was mountain climbing in Jamaica. I was then a college senior and cadet. Compared to my three instances of childbirth pains, the headache preceding my ruptured brain aneurysm was the worst pain I have ever experienced.

I recalled after some of the agony of childbirth, there was always the thrill of seeing the little person who was playing, football, tennis, badminton, hula-hoop or extreme sports for the better part of nine months in my womb. It was sheer pleasure seeing the little darlings. I would count their fingers and toes and check out parental resemblances.

What a difference with the aneurysm! I did not know why I was hurting almost to the point of madness. When the doctors discovered what I "birthing," I was totally unaware of what took place to correct it. Correcting a ruptured aneurysm, like giving birth, is no child's play, and in both instances the result could be devastating. In both situations, the results could be fatal, or it could be permanently disabling.

One doctor said I had amnesia. He said I talked much about many things, including my husband. I felt happy at this point and perked my ears to hear what I said. I asked him to tell me.

He said, "It is better not to hear it."

"Was it that bad? I felt dreadful.

"No, but it is better not to hear it. Use your energy to get well."

"You are right. Thanks!"

Others, whom I had asked to fill in the missing pieces to my puzzle, had reserved their right to withhold from me the things I said and did during my intermittent amnesia. I had to accept their silence because I believed all of them had my best interest in their view.

I realized, during my period of amnesia in the hospital, once again I was a "babbling brook" (Lipsett-Jackson, 2008) as I had become after the first ruptured brain aneurysm sixty-nine days before the second rupture. Witnesses told me I sang, prayed, danced and talked about my husband. I cannot recall any of these behaviors. I learned from the doctors' answers to my questions that amnesia for some or all events is one of the effects of injury to the brain.

Life-style Helps or Hinders

I answered their many questions concerning my life-style, personal and family medical histories. The doctors agreed I did not appear to have the classical risk factors, which normally would have led to brain aneurysms. I am a vegetarian, who eats no animal flesh. Additionally, I had low body weight, and I have never smoked. We did not discuss congenital factors in details. Actually I thought there were none to consider.

Where was it detected?

Its was detected in the Posterior Communicating Artery (PcomA)

The surgeons explained, with the aid of a diagram, the Posterior Communicating Artery (PcomA) originates in the Internal Carotid Artery (ICA) and connects the middle cerebral arteries with the Posterior Cerebral Arteries (PCA). I do not pretend to have understood it then. After general reading and research, I have learned more about the structure of the brain and how aneurysms are formed.

How was my aneurysm detected? I learned it was detected through various high tech tests: Computerized Tomography (CT Scan), which can detect bleeding in the brain; Computerized Tomography Angiogram (CTA), which is more definitive than a CT Scan in detecting bleeds. The most invasive of the tests is a Cerebral Angiogram (CA), which is effective in detecting small aneurysms. The CA also has the greatest risks of all the tests.

My disturbing acquaintance with the Cerebral Angiogram was through a painful swelling in my groin. One night, I experienced a sudden surge of excruciating pain in my groin. My doctor explained the rising and pain in my groin resulted from the insertion of a catheter through my groin to my brain to see what was happening in the arteries.

They injected iodine dye into the arteries through the catheter to facilitate the process. They told me this was how the Cerebral Angiogram was done. Generally, patients are awake for this procedure, but I do not remember undergoing this test. Through this procedure, they were able to see I had a "retrograde bleed".

Can doctors treat an aneurysm before it ruptures?

Yes. If doctors detect an aneurysm early, they can treat it before it ruptures. My sister Irene had brain surgery to correct a ruptured brain aneurysm in 2000. I was still in Hong

Kong then and was not sure what kind of surgery she had. In 2003, a Cerebral Angiogram revealed another aneurysm was forming. Her neurosurgeon operated and prevented the aneurysm from rupturing. One surgeon told me there is a twenty-five percent chance I will have another brain aneurysm; therefore, it is important for me to have a check up annually for early detection.

Some Noticeable Effects

One of the first signs of how the ruptures had affected my brain was my loss of short-term memory. Over brief periods, I could not remember what someone told me, or what I had said to some one. I would ask for or give the same information repeatedly. Someone, sensing I needed some mnemonic device to help me regain my short-term-memory, brought me books to read and writing tablets and a red notebook.

Oh! Oh!

Since I was used to journaling daily, I thought resuming this activity would be just great. When I began to write for the first time after surgery, I was grateful to know I was still able to write my Jamaican-style cursive-large, legible and fancy. At first, I just scribbled lines and letters to stimulate movement in my hands.

Loss of Orthographical Power

I like sophisticated vocabulary like *"orthography"*, which simply means, **"a system of spelling"**. When I decided to write sentences, I discovered I was not able to recall some familiar words, nor could I spell some simple words. One of my sentence was, "I am *aheah* from home." I looked at *aheah* and knew it was wrong. I took forever trying to decipher it. I could not. I borrowed the dictionary from the nurse's station to check my spelling. I could not find the word *aheah.*

I even had problems remembering how to look for a word using the alphabetical order of the dictionary. I was too embarrassed to ask someone to spell such a simple word for me since I believed I spelled excellently. It took me quite a while to figure out *"a-h-e-a-h"* was my post- surgical way of spelling *"away".* I had the biggest and heartiest laugh at myself.

Now, I love to tell children in America my story and ask them to guess how I might have misspelled *"away"* after my brain surgery. It is always hilarious hearing them guess. None ever come close to *"a-h-e-a-h" as my* misspelling for *"away".* The children and I are always amused. We always laughed hilariously at this big spelling blooper I made after my brain surgery. I had a spelling bug. I could not have entered a "Spelling Bee" contest at that point.

Another troubling effect of my ruptured brain aneurysm and brain surgery is neurological deficits. I sometimes had difficulty in processing what others said. For a while, I would hear people speak, but could not fully understand what they were saying. It was almost as if I were deaf.

Often, depending on the speakers, I would ask them to repeat what they said. I would sometimes have to repeat aloud what I heard and try to understand it before responding. Many times, the speaker had to reword the statement or question more simply. My delayed processing of information used to make me feel foolish and frustrated.

Overall physical weakness and lack of coordination, which prevented me from sitting or standing for more than a few minutes, was another effect of my illness. Most of the time was lying. I felt empty and scattered within. I felt my life had lost its purpose.

Is Brain Aneurysm Hereditary?

It is possible to inherit a congenital condition, which predisposes one to brain aneurysm?

I believe the answer is yes.

After returning to America, I remembered a chapter in my mother's medical history: Mabelle had a massive cerebral hemorrhage in 1986 when she was seventy – three years old. The doctors felt they could not help her. After many days in the hospital, everyone thought she would not survive. The doctors would not consider surgery as an option.

Her primary care physician told me he could only leave her in God's hands, for short of a miracle, she would not survive. I thanked him. They sent her home from the hospital to pass, what they thought would have been, her last days at home. They gave her no hope of recovery.

She was as stiff as board and totally dependent on others for her care. She cried although she appreciated the help she got from her children, relatives, friends and home health aides. After two weeks of dependent living, my mother got up one night and shocked everyone by walking. Despite not receiving any aggressive surgical intervention for her cerebral hemorrhage, she survived until 2005.

My sister and I have also survived double massive cerebral aneurysms. Irene had two surgeries. I had two ruptures and one surgery. We are concerned about our daughters. We hope they will learn from their grandmother and from us and become educated about this "silent killer. If they are vigilant of they health and attuned to their bodies, they, too, will survive brain aneurysms. They might be able to escape having any. This is my prayer.

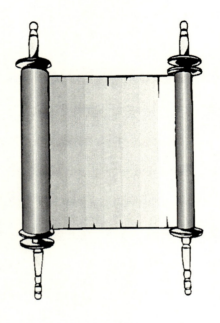

"There was never a moment when I suffered the
indignity
of exposure because of inadequate or poorly
designed hospital gowns."

31

"Living" At Princess Margaret
❧

M y hospital stay lasted thirty days from November 24 to December 24. In the United States, this spans Thanksgiving and Christmas Eve. Princess Margaret Hospital was becoming home for me. During this period, I was in and out of awareness of where I was and what was happening to me. I was vaguely aware of being in the intensive care unit and met a gentle Chinese woman, who also had brain surgery. Later I met her again on the adult medical ward where they accommodated patients recovering from brain surgery and needing physical therapy.

After Brain Surgery

Seven days after successful surgery to clip a ruptured aneurysm in the posterior communicating artery of my brain, my life was still hanging precariously in the balance. The waves of pain, less severe than the pre-surgery head-aches, were persistent. I wondered why they had not stopped completely after surgery. Later, the doctors told me I would have headaches for months after surgery, but I should not worry about having more ruptured aneurysm.

Liberating Discovery

Doctors and nurses came frequently to see me. It seemed inevitable. My medical chart was kept on a high table by my bedside. The doctors and nurses wrote their notes in my presence. Each time they came in, they would ask if how I was feeling and if I needed any thing. I never had to call for them. I do not recall seeing a "call button" near my bed.

They performed various procedures and asked me all kinds of questions. I was always lying. I was hooked up to an intravenous machine, which made me feel I was pinned to the bed. Later, I found I was less restricted than I thought. I could get out of bed and walk, with assistance, while rolling the intravenous bag on a castered pole. The discovery was liberating. I could move around and escape using a bedpan. I wished I could have escaped the headaches.

Body Sympathy

As if in sympathy with my head, my knees began to hurt. One night the pain came on suddenly as if two bombs had exploded in my knees. My threshold for pain is usually high, but when these sympathetic bombs exploded in my knees, I moaned, groaned and cried.

At this moment, the telephone rang. It was my husband calling. I was hurting so badly I could speak only for thirty seconds to let him know I was hurting and could not speak for long. Both of us were disappointed our first telephone conversation, since my hospitalization, ended so soon. The excruciating pain had no sympathy and persisted for a while.

The doctors finally prescribed pain relievers for the severe headaches and an analgesic rub to put out the fire from the explosives in my knees. Unbearable! It took several days for comfort to return. It took a little longer for confidence in my improving condition to return.

I asked for another brain scan to rule out another rising aneurysm. My confidence started strengthening after I got the negative results of the scan. I was happy to know no more aneurysms were forming. Two were more than enough!

HOSPITALITY: HONG KONG STYLE

During my thirty days stay in Princess Margaret Hospital, I received excellent care. The medical team involved with my care gave superior attention to the minutest details of my care. The medical team's performance was always excellent.

I was happily aware of the effort they expended in finding the right combination of foods for my vegetarian diet. The nutrition department initiated frequent talks with me until they found the right foods to satisfy my dietary preference and my medical needs. *I felt the need to "export" this attitude to some American medical facilities, where attention to the substance and quality of patients' nutrition is sadly lacking.*

Another concept, there were so many, I wanted to export was the hospital attire. I said before, I could make a fashion statement with the garment consisting of an attractive plaid pajamas and a solid contrasting, quilted jacket. *There was never a moment when I suffered the indignity of exposure because of inadequate or poorly designed hospital gowns. I resolved to design attire for hospitals in the West in the near future.*

Something on which I could put no price tag was the respect, encouragement and pastoral care I received in Princess Margaret Hospital. I can say these, more than anything else in the hospital environment, enhanced the "miracle" of the risky brain surgery and aided in my speedy and remarkable recovery. The result is a huge miracle!

I was thinking I would have to spend a lifetime paying for thirty days of the most effective care, which began with emergency surgery to "clip" a ruptured brain aneurysm and ended with the best in physical therapy. I concluded if I had to spend two lifetimes paying the millions of dollars it is worth, so be it. The best is never adequately compensated.

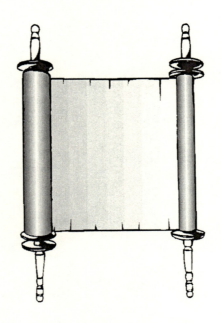

"It was here that the light came shining through.
The windows of my mind were slowly opening to
the light of restored memory.
Gradually, I was remembering past events and
becoming aware of
new happenings, people, things and places within
the hospital."

32

Days Of Light

I continued to become more aware of my environment. I was in the ward for survivors of craniotomy. My closest ward mate was a teenager. I recalled having met a gentle woman who was my roommate in the intensive care unit (ICU). I also remembered meeting her son, who spoke English well. All the other occupants were middle aged to elderly Chinese.

I was the only foreigner. The lesson is – cerebral maladies are not selective. *Everyone, even children, is susceptible.*

Several of the patients, who were brought to this ward for recovery died. The atmosphere was mostly somber.

I wondered about myself since I had no strength to help myself or to move about. I wondered what was I doing in this place.

It was here that the light came shining through. The windows of my mind were slowly opening to the light. Gradually, I was remembering past events and becoming aware of new happenings, people, things and places within the hospital. My awareness was still intermittent.

My Children's Honor

The most delightful event, while at Princess Margaret, was to see two of my three children. One day, I woke up to see my two lovely daughters Jessica and Alaya standing at the foot of my bed. I was sweetly pleased and curiously shocked to see both of them together in Hong Kong. My first question was, "What are you doing here?"

In a chorus they said, "Ma, you are in the hospital; we come to see you."

"Hospital?" I was surprised.

One of them asked, "Do you know where in the world you are?"

That was easy to answer. "Hong Kong." I was confident.

They told me several people had called to say I was critically ill, and at least one person told them I might not make it. They had come to see me at least twice before, but I was not aware of their presence, so I could not recall their visit.

I was disappointed to hear they had visited me early in my hospitalization, but I do not recall seeing them. They were concerned about my amnesia. The way I felt at that moment made me wonder if I had really "made it."

My wondering turned into deep appreciation for my daughters' visit. It was wonderful for me and for others to witness their care and love for me. They had taken leave from their personal affairs, jobs and family *to travel expensively at short notice* from New York and New Jersey to a near dying mother over ten thousand miles away. The risks they took were honoring enough "to raise the dead".

My son Vidal was in Florida working behind the scenes to contact friends in China and relatives and friends in other places. He called often to know about my condition and sent get-well wishes with his sisters.

Their Longevity Wish For Me

My mind flashed to a collage of family photos Vidal, Jessica and Alaya had made as the first Christmas gift to me after their father died suddenly in 1980. We were still a cohesive family after his death. I recalled how my children feared I, too, might die suddenly, leaving them at their tender ages of eleven, eight and five. As if to ensure that did not happen, they called me often at my work place. Their first innocent question was invariably, "Mom are you still here?"

Sometimes I teased them and answered, "No, I am there."

We often laughed at these scenarios. One day, they told me they were praying I would live to be as old as my mother, who was **sixty-seven** when their father died. I reassured them their heavenly Father would answer their prayers.

At the time of my hospitalization, they were young adults, and I was **sixty - four years old**. I was **three years less** than the minimum age they wanted me to reach before dying. At the time of writing my story, I am **sixty-nine years old**. I am

two years older than the minimum age for which they had prayed. This exceeded their expectations. Here they were at my bedside in Princess Margaret Hospital in Hong Kong on the other side of the world. "Thank you Life!"

I was always concerned about the distance between us in case of emergencies. My children have always taught me valuable lessons. This time they showed me distance did not prevent them from expressing their love and care for me. I was thrilled to know they cared to make the long trip.

A Mother's Concern

My thrill of seeing my daughters turned to concern for their families. I thought of the great sacrifices they were making to leave their young sons and working husbands to visit me over ten thousand miles away as well as working behind the scenes to pray and care. Some people may argue that it is their duty to do so. I see their visit as a great honor and not a compulsory duty.

Several of my friends, who met Jessica and Alaya at the hospital, wrote their sentiments in my Red Book. A few follow in abbreviated form:

"Praise God for such wonderful, loving, caring children"

"...Very special to meet your lovely girls!"

"... Such a joy to visit with you and your daughters."

I remembered Alaya was also in Hong Kong earlier, so I asked her if she had not gone home.

She said, "Yes!"

My mind flashed to my second grandson Miles, and how difficult it must have been for Jessica to leave him and her dance studio. I consoled myself with the fact his dad, Mike, is a great "Mr. Mom" as well as a professional photographer, and Miles was "three going on thirty-three"; he could help himself a little.

Alaya also had to leave Jordan with his dad, David, a graphic designer, who is also a great "Mr. Mom". He had much practice since as a fashion designer, Alaya traveled overseas fairly frequently for her job while David cared for

Jordan in her absence. Jordan is also able to help himself. Both grandsons were quite precocious for their ages.

Undoubtedly, I was shocked to see both of my daughters together in Hong Kong for the first time, and it was not a family re-union I had organized. I was becoming confused and a little frightened that something super serious had happened; I was mostly happy and grateful to see them.

Again, they explained someone had called from Hong Kong to say I was gravely ill, and they should come. "So, here we are. You had brain surgery and you are still in the hospital."

"Brain surgery!?" I asked doubtfully. I touched my head and found it was bandaged. I immediately asked, "Where is my hair?"

"It is already growing back". They assured me.

"Hmm!" I thought to myself. "If my hair is already growing back, I must have had brain surgery many days ago. Wow!"

I knew I had been taken to Princess Margaret Hospital but this was my first full awareness of what took place. I had brain surgery! No wonder... I felt as I did – hollow! One of the most important parts of my anatomy had a "booboo"!

I felt I had a gaping hole within me. Something was missing. I was lying on a hospital bed talking with my daughters, but I felt they were fully there, but I was not. A part of me was absent. I understood what they said but still felt disconnected from them and from myself. I just lay there.

At least I was no longer in darkness. *The light had come.* Silently, I rehearsed my awareness of my present situation. I knew I was in the hospital. I had brain surgery, and two of my three children had come to see me. I felt highly honored that both Jessica and Alaya had made tremendous sacrifices to visit me in a hospital over ten thousand miles from New York and New Jersey. They brought get-well wishes and prayers from their brother Vidal, who lives in Florida as well as from other relatives and friends.

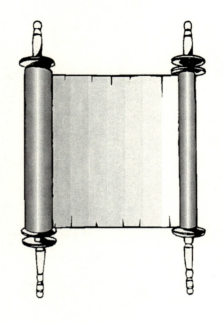

"At that precise moment the figure appeared
to move toward me. Still cradling something, it
stopped at the center of the bed;
bent over me without blocking my vision of my
daughters then disappeared"

33

The Presence

Strange Happening!

Up to the event of my daughters' visit, despite my physical presence in the bed and my awareness of doctors, nurses, therapists, amahs, my daughters, and visitors, I felt I was not all there. I felt split in two whole persons. One was grounded but empty, and one was somewhere out there. I felt part of me had traveled to a distant place and the rest of me would be following soon. I wondered if anyone could see the gaping hole in my center.

Double Talk

While my daughters and I were speaking, I sensed someone else had joined us, but I did not see a third person standing with them at the foot of the bed. Still, I had a strong awareness of having more company. Then I saw something standing behind me. It stood just slightly to the right of my bed head. I could not tell the gender, so I say presence or figure. It was shrouded, and stood with arms bent in front as if cradling a baby or young child or a delicate object. I saw it without turning my head. I kept looking straight at my daughters. It were as if my daughters were one mirror and this mirror reflected the presence behind me.

My Will To Live

I closed my eyes and wondered if I were just imagining things. I opened my eyes again quickly. Suddenly, something strange happened. The presence and I started conversing, but this did not interfere with my conversation with my daughters.

I was aware of communicating with the presence without speaking or hearing distinct words or sentences. It seemed another one of me was talking from some distant place with the Presence by my bedside. How long the discourse lasted I cannot tell. I only knew it ended when I responded,

"I have the will to live. When will you put me back together?"

At that precise moment the figure appeared to move toward me. Still cradling something, it stopped at the center of the bed and bent over me then disappeared. The Presence's visit was brief. Nothing seemed to change physically. I was still lying there. My daughters were still standing there. They did not seem to see anyone, nor did they seem to hear anything. One thing was different. I felt as if I had just returned from a long trip. I heard myself inwardly repeating my response to the presence, *"I have the will to live. When will you put me back together again?"*

Ephiphany?

I felt this confirmed my sense of hollowness and disconnection from others and myself. The questions still unanswered are – did I experience an epiphany, which is described as "the sudden appearance and disappearance of an angel or other heavenly being"? Was I split in two? Was one of me on the bed and the other hovering over me, waiting for the right moment to descend, or the Presence had brought back my life from somewhere else? Did I have an out – of - body experience (OBE)?

I heard of other people, who said they have had an OBE. They spoke convincingly of being split into two separate persons of the same personality. On a television show several years ago, a woman said she could observe herself that had been seriously injured or had died lying helplessly, while another person like her hovered over the helpless body. I am not sure what was happening to me, but I felt something significant was taking place.

The words of Apostle Paul come to my mind:
I know about one of Christ's followers, who was
Taken up into the third heaven about
fourteen years ago.
I don't know if the man was still in the body
when it happened, but only God knows.
As I said, only God really knows if

the man was in the body at the time.

II Corinthians 12:2-3 (CEV)

Well, I felt only God knew what I was experiencing. I am confident of having seen a Presence by my bed at the same time my daughters were there.

I believe firmly in the reality of ministering spirits. According to the Holy Scriptures, there are ministering spirits sent to serve those who will inherit salvation (Hebrews 1:14 KJV). I might have seen several ministering angels in the persons of friends, nurses, doctors and my daughters, who were sent to Princess Margaret Hospital in Hong Kong to carry out a divine decree.

It is difficult for me to grasp the reality of an epiphany, but it is quite realistic to testify something had gone terribly wrong with my health. Something had threatened my life. My dependence on God paid huge dividends. He said, "No." to my death. He allowed me to survive two ruptured brain aneurysms in Discovery Bay, Hong Kong, within sixty-nine days. He flawlessly appointed caring people to minister to me in my darkest moments of amnesia. I made it in time to the hospital to have corrective brain surgery after a forty- minute commute through some of Hong Kong's busiest streets. **No sneezes for this double miracle, no doubts, no second-guesses, only perpetual, highest praises!**

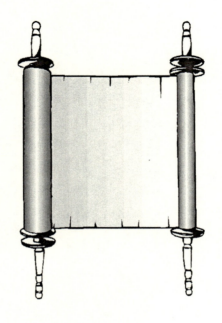

"Forever I will say and sing:

Blessed is the Lord for He has shown me

His marvelous kindness in a strong city.

Psalm 31:21."

34

The Morning After

The morning after the appearance of the presence, I felt very different. I had the best sleep in days without analgesic massage to relieve the pain in my legs and without sleeping aid. When I awoke, an important first happened. Actually, it was a group of firsts. I felt whole. No longer was there a gaping hole in the center of my being. I felt knitted together. The feelings of disconnection had all disappeared. I lay quietly for a while to get accustomed to the restored feeling of well being. I could not fully grasp the reasons for the sudden changes but I welcomed them.

From the day I became fully aware of where I was and the fact I had to be there for many days, I tried to resume some of me pre-hospitalization activities. **The pre-dawn activities of greatest importance to me were biblical studies, prayers, meditation, physical exercise and journaling.**

As soon as I could, I began rising at my usual early hour of 4:00 a.m. to pray, meditate and journal for sixty to ninety minutes. Then I went walking for thirty to sixty minutes. I got permission from my doctors and nurses to leave my floor. I walked up and down, round and about on the floors of the building in which I was stationed. I also walked along the promenade connecting the two major buildings of Princess Margaret Hospital. From the promenade, I could see the outside of the hospital. It was a pleasant reprieve from staying in doors.

My close spiritual encounters during my hospital sojourn were obviously different from my previous experiences. They were strange, rich and cathartic (cleansing). I was overflowing with gratitude. I felt compelled to write. My journal entry for the fourteenth day of my hospitalization follows:

Journal entry of December 07, 2002

FIRSTS

Today is a day of firsts for which I am deeply grateful. I thank you Lord!

This is the first morning after the first night of no headaches for almost the entire night. It is the first day after consciously speaking with my Lord for extended periods and receiving His directions for troubling situations in my life.

Today is the first day of doing prescribed exercises in bed with the help of instructions and a simple contraption from the physiotherapy department. I felt great! Another first is eating my own raw organic rolled oats with honey and soymilk for breakfast. Yummy, yummy!

A REAL BIG FIRST is having a shampoo, shower, and bath and grooming after breakfast. With shampooed and blown dried hair, clean clothes and deodorized and lotioned body, I felt brand new. Exhilarating!

"Playing the numbers"

*An exciting first is going to the **first- floor** art museum and beautifully manicured gardens with Alaya and "The*

*Director" who visited me for the **first time**. They brought me some delicious **firsts**: extremely sweet Japanese apple, tart cherries and Chinese bananas, which were still ripening.*

*With my visitors' assistance, I had my **first** long walk. These many firsts confirmed it pays to put **God FIRST in my life**. I am on the **fifth** (5). **The 5ᵗʰ floor** reminds me of the **Beatitudes in Matthew 5**. I am indeed BLESSESD. By the way, I am in **bed 41**. This is a constant reminder of **God's sure promises to me in Isaiah 41: 10 – 20**, which Jessica and Alaya read for me two days ago. So many firsts occur this day! Praise God!*

By the end I had to thank God GREATLY for two bowel movements and the elimination of much foul smelling gases and a volume of urine. YUK! These biological functions, which I partially took for granted while well, become great pleasures and accomplishments at this time. I praise you Holy Father!

Even writing this list of first while hospitalized is a BIG FIRST FOR ME. Since it is a testimony of God's care for me, I believe it is very important that I write it.

"Wait!" There is more to come. After meditating and giving thanks for this gift of a peaceful night's sleep, I rose slowly from the bed. I sat on the edge of the bed. I felt strong! Wow! I felt energized.

The urge to urinate came with my excitement. Usually, I would call for a nurse or a nurse's assistant to bring a bedpan for this purpose, or depending on the level of pain I was experiencing, I would ask her to assist me to walk to the bathroom. If I were strong enough I would use a walker. In either case, I would have to remain in the bathroom and signal when I was finished, so someone could escort me back to my bed.

The Bawling Out

Well, the morning after I told the Presence I had the will to live and asked, "When will you put me back together?" was an exception. I felt so strong and confident; I did not ask for assistance to the bathroom. I simply got off the bed and walked there by myself. When the nurse missed me from my bed, they looked for me and found I had gone to the bathroom unaided. After asking if I was okay, the nurse sternly told me,

"Don't do that again! Tell someone when you want to go or ask for the bedpan. You could fall. Do you understand?!"

*"YES!" I understood, but I felt I had graduated from using bedpans and from asking for assistance to get to the bathroom. Something special had happened the night before. Now, I felt whole. There was no more gaping hole in the center of my being. **I was back together again!** I had walked independently for the first time since my surgery.*

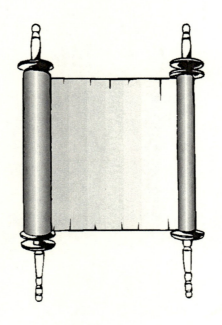

"To get through this exercise,

I pretended I was playing an organ the way I

had seen my cousin Florence Thomas (Bliss) and

other organists play."

35

The Miracle Of Recovery

Physiotherapy Musical

After my dramatic first of walking independently in the adult recovery ward at P.M.H., I started receiving an effective regimen of physical therapies. This was also a first in my life. To maximize my rehabilitation, therapy was scheduled twice a day – early in the day after breakfast with a rest period between and in the afternoon after lunch with a rest period. If I were unable to go to physiotherapy center for any reason, the therapist would come to me and do a modified form of therapy right in my bed. Once I started therapy, I did not miss a day.

Sometimes the exercises were challenging enough to reduce me to tears. I was amazed at my inability to understand and follow the instructions of the therapist. I became more frustrated when I understood the instruction, but I could not get my body to respond appropriately and do the exercise. Several times I felt like a real idiot at not being able to do simple physical tasks, which I believed young children would find easy.

One day, I decided to meet every challenge. I was motivated by the fact I had survived when others perished; I would honor their memory with a "concert." On this day, my therapist introduced new equipment to me. I call it the "lathe." I had to sit and move it with my feet as if I were treading a sewing machine. It reminded me of the pedal on a pipe organ although the foot movements were not as elaborate.

To get through this exercise, I pretended I was playing an organ I had seen my cousin Florence (Bliss) and other organists play. I visualized them playing, and I started singing quietly in my corner. The work became easier. I sang in memory of those who did not survive to face the challenges of recovery through physical therapy. I sang songs of praises I recalled or made up. My singing led me to praying. Soon tears were flowing - tears of mixed emotions – regret and gratitude.

The therapist heard my sobs and offered facial tissues for my tears. She asked if I was hurting. When I answered, "No," she placed a comforting hand on my shoulder and said, "I understand." Although I did not think she or anyone else fully understood my depth of gratitude and appreciation for being alive, it was reassuring to hear her words, "I understand".

Even now as I edit this section, I am tearfully grateful for the miracle of my recovery from the life threatening illness of ruptured brain aneurysms. It is impossible for me to remember without shedding tears of appreciation. My "concert" continued for a while longer. It ended when the therapist signaled a change from physical therapy to occupational therapy.

I also received occupational therapy to regain the ability to resume activities of daily living (ADL) such as cooking, shopping and personal hygiene. The therapists covered all bases. I was amazed at the extent to which the physiotherapy and the medical departments went to facilitate my recovery. They literally, "Left no stones unturned."

My therapist was truly encouraging. She incorporated make-believe, pretending and imagining into the exercises to make them fun and challenging. Quite often, I laughed heartily because of some of the occupational therapies we did.

In one of our occupational therapy sessions, she gave me several rolls of play dough with which to "cook" creatively. I decided to "cook" a meal and invite her to share it with me. The meal was totally vegetarian. She wanted some meat. She said I tricked her. We laughed happily.

As my physical and occupational therapist, she showed interest in every aspect of my recovery. She complimented my effort and encouraged me to be consistent. When she met Alaya, she told her I was, "saving my own life". I told her she was divinely appointed to assist me in the process of my recovery.

She wrote in my Red Book, *"I am happy to see you having a wonderful recovery. You have shown me your great effort to do well. All is your effort. Hope you will get well soon"*. PT

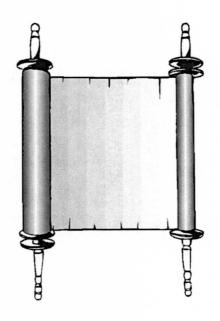

."… I tell you the truth, unless you change and

become like little children,

you will never enter the Kingdom of Heaven."

Matthew 18:3 N.I.V.

36

Extreme Makeover: Spiritual Edition
Part I

My stay in P.M.H. lasted thirty days. As I have stated previously, I was unaware of some of what took place on some days. I was sufficiently aware of the conclusion that as serious as my condition was, this was not just a matter of first fainting in a prayer meeting then sixty-nine days later becoming suddenly ill with the worst headache of my life and having craniotomy to correct a ruptured brain aneurysm. No! This was a carefully orchestrated series of events to accomplish my extreme makeover – spiritual edition.

Prior to returning to Hong Kong on September 05, 2002, I had started on a path to spiritual renewal. I had become deeply dissatisfied with my life as it was then, and with my lackluster worship experiences. I yearned for more dynamic worship encounters and opportunities to serve others spontaneously and unceremoniously.

I longed to see the gospel of Christ expressed practically to meet the various needs of the individual and the communities of the needy without any of the oppressive type of mentality characteristic of governmental poverty relief programs. I wanted to go about "doing good" with the compassion and simplicity, which Christ exemplified.

How shall I accomplish this? I returned to Hong Kong with a strong desire for a better spiritual condition and richer worship encounters. I realized the change I desired had to begin with me. It had to be internal and spiritual.

An "Emmaus Road" experience of weekly biblical study led by the presiding priest of the DB Anglican Church; another study with a group of women in Peninsula Village, DB and the weekly prayer meeting in the Greens were the catalysts. Getting involved in the church's prison ministry was, and still is, one of the practical ways of "going about doing good."

BECOMING A CHILD AGAIN

It was at Princess Margaret Hospital in Kowloon, Hong Kong that the ultimate transformation in miraculous magnitude happened. I kept seeking avenues of meaningful changes. I searched the scriptures. One of the passages I revisited several times follows:

I tell you the truth, unless you change and become like little children, you will never enter the Kingdom of Heaven Matthew 18:3 NIV

This masterful admonition prefaced the answer I would get for how to accomplish the drastic, inner change I desired and how to "go about doing good" without the restrictive shackles of my own preconceived notions. I HAD TO BECOME A CHILD AGAIN!

I felt a little like Nicodemus, who wondered if he had to enter again in his mother's womb in order to be born again (John 3:1-21).

How was I to change meaningfully? Nothing short of becoming a child again would do.

Sixty-four Year Old Juvenile

After several days in the adult recovery ward, the doctors transferred me to the neurological-pediatric ward. This made me the oldest "child" there. Compared to the juvenile patients, I was Methuselah, son of Enoch (Genesis 5:21), although I will not live for "969 years." The purpose of the transfer was not explained, but it delighted me. I thought if I am with children, perhaps, I would have an opportunity to watch the physical "resurrection" I experienced earlier in my own recovery. Perhaps their innocence would become contagious, and I would learn what it means to change and become like a child again, not just to "enter Heaven", but I would know how to serve with true humility on earth. I welcomed the possibilities.

"God is after me!"

When I entered the ward, a father was holding an infant on his shoulder. The child's head was bandaged. The father was patting the child's back and swaying from side to side as if comforting or hushing him to sleep. The sight was one of a child's total dependence on his father and the father's devoted, tender care for the child. I found this picture captivating and meaningful to me. I felt I needed comfort, too.

I starting singing "Jesus loves the little children, all the children of the world...." The father spun around. He was still patting his son's back. The child clung, face down, to his father's shoulder. The father faced me. He seemed a bit startled. He looked at me closely and exclaimed "You, too?! I was a puzzled at his exclamation.

I asked, "What do you mean?"

"Are you a Christian?" He asked me.

"Yes." My answer was brief.

"You are the second person, whom I have met this week, who is a Christian. I think God is after me!"

"How so? I waited a while for his answer.

"Well, the first person is a friend, who has been telling me I need to serve God. I want to do that. I want my whole family and me to serve God." I listened with deep interest. He continued.

"I gave my two sons biblical names and I took "David" as my English name. I wanted to follow God, but look what happened!" He sounded frantic. "My older son has Learning Disabilities, and now, my younger son had an accident that required brain surgery. The surgeons said he may develop seizures. I do not know what to do. I feel like this is all unfair. Here you come singing that song to my son. *I believe God is after me!*"

I did not quite know how to respond to this dad, so I turned my attention to his son, who had finally raised his head from his dad's shoulder. He looked at me suspiciously. I played briefly with him then went to my assigned bed. It felt asinine being in a pediatric ward, especially now that I am viewed as helping God "chase" this bewildered Father.

My Precious Room mates

The juvenile patients were two infants. One was only four months old. He had extra fluid in his cranium cavity. This made his head too large for his small body to support. Doctors call this "Hydrocephalus". They could not prop him up to sit, so he had to lie all the time. He had brain surgery to reduce the fluid in his head.

The older infant was seven months old. He was the boy his father was holding when I entered the pediatric ward. He had fallen from his carriage, while his amah was caring for him. He sustained head injuries that required brain surgery. His father told me the Hong Kong authorities were investigating the accident. This added to their grief.

I was particularly drawn to these two infants. They became precious to me. They were so vulnerable and helpless. I wished they did not have to suffer such pain.

I asked the parents, who had become "residents" at their sons' cribs, if I might pray for them. They agreed for my prayers for their sons but refused prayers for themselves. I arose at 4:00 a.m. each morning to pray quietly for the children while they were sleeping.

For a while, the two infants and I were the only patients in the pediatric-neurological ward. Later, some older children entered the ward almost on a daily basis and remained overnight or a day or two for observation. Several of them spoke English or Mandarin, so I was able to communicate with them. I taught them several children's games. Soon, we were calling each other by first names. They called me constantly, "Tmay, Tmay, come play!"

Their parents often reminded them I was an adult and they should respect me. I could see their disappointment when their parents insisted they should leave me alone. The parents did not know I had become a child again, and their little tykes were my playmates. I told them, through an interpreter, I did not mind playing with their children. The parents relaxed a bit, but they still kept a watchful eye to make sure the children were behaving well.

The atmosphere was lively here. The children were sometimes crying, yelling, laughing, screaming, shouting, talking, singing or playing. Some children, who were too ill for any of the above, just moaned. This setting, although depressing at times, suited me.

It reminded me of my own childhood joys and pains. It was a fresh reminder of the joys and pains of my children and grandchildren. It was wonderful to hear the children's laughter.

Playing and interacting with the children had a positive rejuvenating effect on both my mind and body. I felt well and energized. I was inspired to rise early and resume my power walks and to begin journaling again.

DVT Candidate?

During one of my walks, I stopped to read the attractive bulletin board. The colorful, well - written display on Deep Vein Thrombosis (DVT) interested me. This was my first time hearing of this. The author spoke of how likely it is for patients, who had brain surgery, to develop blood clots and seizures. I became concerned. Since the author was one of my doctors, I spoke with him about this. He ran some tests and assured me I would not developed DVT. I felt relieved.

Re-united

While walking around on the neurological floor, I met my former I.C.U. roommate. She was across from me in the adult surgical ward. She needed encouragement to take walks. Her feet were dry and a little stiff, so she was afraid to walk. With the permission of her medical team and her son, whom I had met earlier, I became one of her visitors. They also gave permission for me to massage her feet and invite her to walk with me. She accepted my invitation. We enjoyed many early morning jaunts.

Changes

Being in the pediatric - neurological ward was beginning to have a profound effect on me. I felt I was losing much of my adult inhibitions and false pride. I was beginning to think more simply and selflessly. My attitude was less expectant and demanding of others.. I did whatever I could to help myself and made it easier for the staff to do pay attention to the children. Before going for my early morning walks, I made my bed and tidied the ward. When I returned, I attended independently to my personal hygiene. I looked for opportunities to help the children, their parents and other patients.

One of the doctors commented in my Red Book. "We love to have you here to share your wonderful experience with our patients. Nice if I see you again. Dr._"

This comment was both humbling and encouraging.

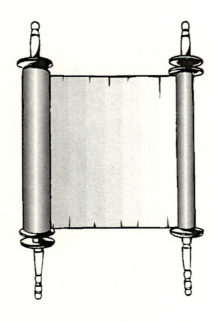

"I felt as if someone wrote this book especially

for me.

The effects were visceral, cathartic and

transforming"

37

Extreme Makeover:
Spiritual Edition
Part II

The Transformation

A Special Book

A friend from DB, sensing my need for reading materials, sent me a package consisting of tracts, book-
lets and a small book. Ironically, or appropriately, the book
was about "worship". I cannot recall the exact title or author,
but a children's ministry in Malaysia produced it.

Although I needed reading materials, I decided to share
with the children, their parents, the staff and all who would

accept my offers. I tried repeatedly to give away the book about worship to someone. Everyone refused it. When there was no taker, I decided to read the book.

After reading only a few pages, I was greatly moved by its content. I devoured it quickly then read again more slowly to fully grasp its meaning. The author focused on true worship from a child's perspective. I was amazed at the detailed discussion on how to use God's redemptive names in acts of worship. I was equally surprised the material was meant for children.

I had learned about these divine names as an adult, but I certainly received no specific directions for incorporating them in acts of worship. Here, in the neurological-pediatric ward of Princess Margaret Hospital in Hong Kong, I was learning for the first time from a child's perspective how to incorporate them in my spiritual life. *I felt as if someone wrote this book especially for me. The effects were visceral, cathartic and transforming.*

Each name was powerfully engaging. Each time I read one, meditated on it and tried to incorporate it in my prayers,

I wept. What it meant to me to learn about meditating on and using the Hebrew names of God in acts of worship would fill a large book.

I will only list some of the names and their simply meanings in "A WORD ABOUT…" at the end of this book.

"Pray On Your Bed"!

I often knelt to pray after my meditation. One morning, a nurse found me on my knees. It startled her. She was concerned. She thought I had fallen off the bed. She rushed to me and held me under both arms from behind and pulled me up. "Are you hurt, are you hurt?"

I answered, "No! Thank you. I am praying."

Her concern turned to discipline. She scolded me.

"Next time, pray on your bed!" This was good advice, but I am not sure I followed it. I continued to kneel and pray for the infants when this nurse was not around.

A Special Invitation

While I was on the children's ward, several nurses and doctors spoke with me socially. They wanted to know about my family and how and why I came to Hong Kong. One

Tuesday, someone invited me to a Christian fellowship after lunch. Some members of the nursing staff organized the noon - time prayer gathering. They met twice weekly to fellowship and to pray. I was surprised they invited me. I gladly accepted the invitation.

They gathered in another building across the street from the one I was in. There was no need for me to change my clothing. The beautiful hospital attire was attractive enough to wear outside the ward. I applied make-up and earrings to complete the "fashion statement." Vanity!

CHANGED

Attending the prayer gathering was a refreshing addition to my already interesting and fruitful hospital stay. I was quite surprised I was the designated "guest speaker" that day. Previously, I would have minded the impromptu request and would have felt "put upon" by others. I would have felt uneasy speaking at such short notice. This time, I felt prepared. I spoke freely of my miraculous experiences before and since my admission to Princess Margaret Hospital.

During my talk with the nurses, I experienced a deep calm. My heart felt new. I felt my close encounter with death and my hospitalization had transformed me into a humbler, wiser woman. Once again, I realized my near-death experience was not just for me. I believe it was divinely orchestrated to bring me in contact with others for a specific purpose.

I was beginning to think there was indeed a real purpose for me to be in the hospital and especially to be among the children. It may take years for me to fully know. **I confidently say the children's neurological ward of Princess Margaret Hospital in Hong Kong was where my amazing transformation from a spiritually and physically sick adult to a well, vibrant living "child" started. It is here that the road to true compassion, kindness, humility and patience began. I believe I was beginning to learn how to go about "doing good without the restrictions of my own preconceived notions".**

After the gathering, members of the group visited me in the children's ward. They talked and played with the children. I was delighted to hear them talking and laughing so happily. That same day, I had other visitors. They included my rescuers and the priest from the Anglican Church in Discovery Bay and two officers from the Citizens Services of the American Embassy in Hong Kong. They brought me the loveliest and largest pink roses I have ever seen.

Playing Games

Some adults brought games to play with me. My all time favorite was Scrabble. I was happy I did not forget how to play well enough to win several games. I felt my spelling was moving a long way from *"Aheah"*. This was how I spelled *"away"* in the early days of my recovery. My opponents did not mind my beating them at Scrabble. They were happy for the improvement in my spelling.

Before the visitors left, they wrote in my Red Book. One wrote:

"Dear Tmay,

Nice to hear your testimony and all the goodness of God's work on your life. Let us glorify God for He is worthy to be praised and honored. Your sharing is just what I need at this time. I thank God for placing you here. I need His assurance. I thank you for your willingness to be used by God. God blessings to you and your family."

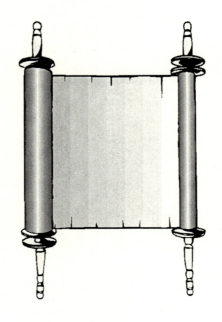

"The Lord preserves the simple.

I was brought very low and He helped me.

Psalm 116:6"

38

Time To Go Home

Eyes on The "Child"

One day, two of the children and I were playing "tic-tac-toe." I noticed several staff members were observing us. I felt strongly they were watching me. I wondered why.

Members of the hospital administration visited the ward often. There was much surveillance and discussions. The movements in and out of the children's ward increased. In my second week there, they moved in three other adults, including my former I.C.U. roommate. That same day they moved them out. I was the only adult "juvenile" left.

I did not know what caused the quick entries and exits. Later, I learned the general opinion was I appeared too well to remain longer in the hospital. They wanted my bed for a sicker adult. I wanted to leave the hospital. Since I had no family in Hong Kong, I was concerned about living alone so soon after brain surgery. One doctor told me it was not advisable.

Pack Your Stuff

The plan was to transfer me back to the adult ward. My nurse told me to pack for the transfer. I did. I FELT SAD to be leaving the children with whom I had bonded so closely. They were now my extended family. I waited for the transportation to take me to the adult ward several buildings away. I waited, but none came. Instead, a group of administrators came.

The "Press Conference" and Exhibition

They surrounded my bed. First, the leader addressed the group in Cantonese. Then he pointed to me as if I were **"Exhibit A"** and said in English, "Look at her! He pointed to a male staff and said, "She is like him." He pointed to a female staff and said, "She is like her." Lastly, he pointed to himself and said, "She is like me."

The triple comparison baffled me. He continued. "She is walking, writing, laughing, playing with the children. She is well! She is well! She needs to go home! He was emphatic. "We need sick people in here. She is not sick. We need to fill these beds!"

Rare Opportunity

I listened in wonderment. Why was I on exhibition? Why was it necessary to surround me with so many members of the staff? "Ah!" Suddenly, I saw the "bigger picture". I thought: whatever the intent, this was the perfect opportunity to see all or most of the dedicated people, who cared so well for me and to thank them. I raised my hand and asked the administrator if I may speak. He gave me permission. I thanked him and all his staff for the remarkable surgery and their care, which saved my life. Then I respectfully asked if any of them had had brain surgery. I told him of my reluctance to return home before my daughter Alaya returned to take me home.

The administrator asked, "Of what are you afraid?"

I hesitated then I said, "I just don't want to be alone."
The doctor, who had called my daughters twice, spoke. "Her
daughter is returning on December 27th."

CONFIRMING A MIRACLE

The chief surgeon expressed his joy at my remarkable
recovery. He then told me, "You are fortunate. We saw dried
blood when we operated. This means you could have died
from the first rupture".

At that moment, I realized the chief surgeon was
unknowingly confirming the occurrence of a miracle in my
life. He and his medical team were eyewitnesses and active
participants. For me to have survived two ruptured cerebral
aneurysms, when most people do not usually survive one, is
nothing short of double miracles. I was awed.

The Administrator was quiet.

Then he asked me, "Do you think this is a hotel or a
motel?"

Before I could respond, he said, "If you were in America,
they would have kicked you out long ago!"

"Ouch!"

His statement was truthful and informative. He and his team had done their best for me, and now he wanted me out. Among other reasons, I was in his department and he wanted me to leave since I appeared well enough to go home. I did not know how to respond, so I kept silent. I risked giving him the impression I agreed with him totally.

Then I remembered one of my former students from Mainland China would be visiting me before Alaya returned. I told him this.

"When is she coming?" He asked while writing.

I told him she would arrive on December 23rd and would come to see me on December 24th. Another person asked if she could take care of me until Alaya returned.

I said, "Yes! I am sure she would not mind."

Unpack Your Stuff

The administrator spoke to his team. "Okay! That's five days away. She can stay for five days but no longer!" He was serious.

Someone asked if he should transfer me back to the adult ward. His answer was quick and definite. "No! She is going nowhere! Do not transfer her. Let her stay here for the five days and do whatever she wants!"

Press Conference Ended

"Wow!" The exhibition and press conference were over, and I had a big smile on my face and much joy in my heart. The administrator had just given me a gift of precious time to spend however I wanted.

The Show Went On

The Physiotherapy Department continued giving me physical therapy. I continued my early morning walks with my ex room mate, my journaling and praying for the children and their parents.

An Unexpected Request

Two of the parents asked if they could speak with me about the Bible. I was happy to hear their request. They included their domestic helper. I told them I would be delighted. Sometimes, twice a day we had discussions. Before I left the children's ward, they told me they had decided to become

Christians. I was overjoyed to hear this. I was more over-joyed when I heard them telling others in the hospital about their decision. I prayed for a bright future for this family

Cold Feet

I was already having separation jitters about leaving the children and their parents, who had become my family for the greater part of my thirty days stay in Princess Margaret Hospital.

The day before Christmas Eve, a large group from a local church came to the hospital for an annual Christmas celebration. They stopped by the children's ward and gave them gifts. Then they read the Christmas story and sang many traditional Christmas Carols.

This was a joyous celebration. We took group photos of everyone. I thought it was a "grand finale to my stay, but I was having "cold feet" about leaving Princess Margaret Hospital that had been my real home for thirty days.

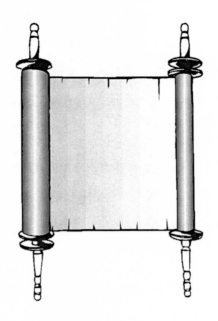

With all my heart I praise the Lord,

and with all that I am I praise His holy name!

With all my heart I praise the Lord!

I will never forget how kind He has been.

The Lord forgives our sin;

heals us when we are sick and protects us from death.

His kindness and His love are a crown on our heads.

Each day that we live he provides for our needs

and gives us the strength of a young eagle.

Psalm 103: 1-5 CEV

39

Leaving Princess Margaret Hospital

Gracie is Coming! Gracie is Coming!

On the eve of Christmas Eve 2002, my friend Gracie from Dalian, China, came to visit with me. On Christmas Eve, two of my neighbors from DB accompanied her to escort me home from Princess Margaret Hospital. I felt I was leaving home instead of going home.

It was a dear honor for me to have a former student to visit me in one of my darker moments. I first met Gracie in summer 1995 during my first trip to China. She and I became friends and sisters. We kept in touch constantly.

When Gracie arrived to take me home, I started experiencing separation anxiety from the children to whom I had become attached. I took pictures with them and their parents and exchanged addresses. I bequeathed the exotic roses from the American Embassy to the workstation shared by the doctors and nurses.

Letters Of Gratitude

I wrote "Thank you's" to the departments, which cared for me. I wrote individual letters of gratitude to the surgeons, who saved my life and to the administrator, who had given me such a generous gift of time to regain my confidence of living alone.

HUGE SURPRISE

The last step before leaving the hospital was to go to the business office. My friends escorted me there on foot. Amazing! What a contrast to when I entered the hospital unaware of everything! Now, I could walk. I was coherent. I was fully aware of what was happening around me.

I gave the cashier the discharge papers. She presented me with a bill. *I expected a six-figure bill. Instead, to my greatest surprise, it was the equivalent of two hundred and fifty-five American dollars.* Getting copies of the notes for the thirty days, cost more than the actual stay. How could it have cost so little for thirty days of hospitalization? I thought surely they had made a huge mistake. They had not.

The Hong Kong Immigration Department had granted me an "endorsement" and an investment visa to set up a "sole proprietorship" business in Hong Kong. The endorsement came through while I was still in the Hospital on December 05, 2002. The hospital administrator had treated me as an "entitled person" and charged me accordingly.

My friend Carrie paid the bill. I accepted it as a loan since Alaya was returning and would reimburse her. When Alaya arrived and withdrew the funds from my account to pay Carrie, she told us she and her husband decided to give it to us as a Christmas present. We were speechless and deeply grateful.

These were another set of "Double Miracles" and a HUGE SURPRISE!!!!!!!!!!!!!!!!

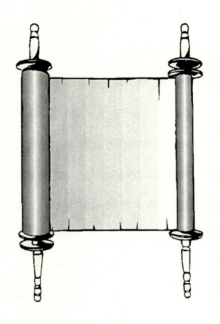

"On April 09, 2008, on "American Idol Give Back", the report of the number of uninsured in America was a staggering fifty million. Children make up a large percentage of this number."

40

Reflections From America

I definitely wanted to export this concept and experience of affordable and excellent healthcare to the United States of America where, if one does not have insurance coverage, "even a brief hospital stay can easily cost tens of thousands of dollars and put one on the edge of bankruptcy." (ABC Television- Healthcare in America Feb. 2003)

I was rudely awakened to this fact when I returned to America. When I had my first medical follow-up in Hong Kong, it was complimentary. After returning to America, one consultation and lab work cost me more than twice as much as my thirty days hospital stay in Hong Kong.

The services included emergency craniotomy, physical therapy, occupational therapy, nutrition, pastoral care, medication, tests, attending physicians and nursing services and all the amenities provided by the Princess Margaret Hospital.

The rudest part of the awakening was the reports of the large numbers of uninsured in America. The most troubling report was about the tens of thousands of critically ill, uninsured patients, who are "allowed to die" each year. (ABC Television Commentary February 2003)

On April 09, 2008, on "American Idol Give Back", the report of the number of uninsured in America was a staggering fifty million. Children make up a large percentage of the number. Many people, including me, are astonished at such outlandish, negative health insurance statistics for the world's greatest nation. Both politicians and civilians must act concertedly to bring about lasting and substantive changes quickly to an ailing health care system.

MIRACLES REDOUBLED

I felt my double miracles in Discovery Bay, Hong Kong were quadrupled. I was an American under sixty-five years of age and without health insurance at the time of my illness. I was convinced after hearing the report on the state of American health care, **"Mercy indeed had said, "No" to my becoming a fatal statistic in America and had transported me to Discovery Bay, Hong Kong for the double miracles.**

Inspired Expressions of Gratitude

In addition to writing my story of this incredible experience, I am hoping for an opportunity to give back something more tangible than new medical dictionaries and children's books to Princess Margaret Hospital Neurological Department. I would like to become proactive in helping to bring about changes in the pediatric neurosurgical ward in which I spent my best and most productive hospitalization. I think the children could benefit from the comforts an extension of this unit would offer. An extension would also enable and the medical personnel, who serve them, to do so with greater ease.

This is just my way of wanting to express my gratitude in a small way for the magnificent work the Neurosurgical Department did to save my life. They turned a potential tragedy, which started on September 19, 2002, in Discovery Bay, Hong Kong, and culminated in brain surgery on November 24, 2002, into a double life-saving miracle for me.

Secondly, this experience has inspired me to research health care systems and contribute in even a small way to the regeneration of the American healthcare, especially for the uninsured seniors under age sixty-five and for single parent families.

This may sound like a David and Goliath story, but we must remember the giant fell! David the shepherd boy in the biblical story, by using the right equipment and focus, prevailed over the menacing giant. (I Samuel 17)

Americans have the ability to conquer the giants of inadequate and no healthcare for millions of her PRECIOUS PEOPLE. With the right combination of validation, knowledge and strategies, Americans can provide the best healthcare for its citizens without anyone experiencing financial disaster or untimely death.

My third inspiration is to investigate the causes and types of aneurysms and make information about signs, symptoms and precautions available to people at risk. I was at risk without knowing because of family medical history.

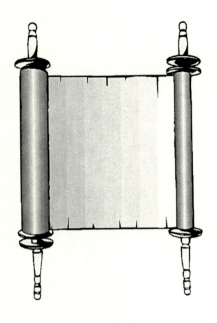

"Finally, I understood what the doctors meant by
their comments about my life style and its relationship to my health.
They were pleased with my active lifestyle
of regular exercise, sensible eating".
meditation, low weight, low body fat and
normal cholesterol and blood pressure levels.

41

A Family Legacy?

It was not until after my life-saving surgery in Hong Kong in 2002, and my return to the United States in 2003, I realized I was genetically predisposed to cerebral hemorrhage or brain aneurysm. The massive bleeding my mother had in her brain in 1986, for which the doctor thought there was no hope of survival, was a warning for my sister Irene and me. In 2001, and 2003 my sister Irene underwent surgeries for brain aneurysms. That was a warning for me. After revisiting these two events, I realized there was a strong genetic *proclivity* to brain aneurysms for my siblings and me. I had two ruptures and one brain surgery in 2002. **These are warnings for my children.**

Life Style Helps

Finally, I understood what the doctors meant by their comments about my life style and its relationship to my health. They were pleased with my active lifestyle of regular exercise, sensible eating, meditation, low weight, low body fat and normal cholesterol and blood pressure levels. They were baffled about my having two bleedings. According to their reasoning, this should not have happened to me.

I drew comfort from their belief it could have been caused by a parasite and not genetics. Narrowing our search for the cause helped me to see more clearly what I was up against. Now, I know how to educate my daughters about aneurysms and the precautions they need to take to protect themselves against this unmerciful, swift, silent killer.

I knew nothing about aneurysms until after a twenty-one year old woman, I knew in Fort Lauderdale suddenly fell while sweeping and died before any help arrived. For several years, as early as 1986, I had been experiencing strange, burning sensations in my head. I did not have severe headaches. I also had series of petit mal after dealing with my mother's severe illness. I would lose awareness of my surroundings and forget my name, the day of the week and my telephone number for split seconds.

I sought medical help. The doctors did brain scans and blood work and found nothing. They thought stress was the underlying factor for the temporary unawareness. I was not prone to having severe headaches, and I knew nothing about migraines, so on November 24, 2002, when a "stubborn bully" showed up and took up residence, I knew it was time, according to my grandsons Jordan and Miles, "To call for the big artillery". I did so by going to the hospital.

Dried Sentinel

After the surgery to save my life, the seriousness of the whole scenario is still baffling me. The Chief Neurosurgeon said he saw dried blood in my brain. This showed there was a previous bleeding, which likely happened when I fainted on September 19, 2002

When I returned to the States, the first neurologist I saw told me the previous bleed is called "sentinel." This bleeding gave me a "wake up call" on September 19, 2002, when I collapsed in the prayer meeting. I did not heed the warning. I did not verify medically the reasons for my collapse. I lived miraculously "death-free" for sixty-nine days until November 24, 2002 when the unbearable headaches started.

Double Miracle Underscored

The facts of having a sentinel bleed; living well for sixty-nine days; having a second bleed – a rupture; surviving the forty minute ambulance ride from DB to Princess Margaret Hospital in Kowloon; surviving brain surgery underscore the enormity and graciousness of divine intervention. Given the potentially fatal nature of cerebral hemorrhage, it **is inconceivable** I would have survived one. To have survived TWO is SUPERNATURAL!!!!

My Creator, whom I have been serving from my youth in Jamaica, has been excellently merciful to me. He indeed performed a double miracle in Discovery Bay, Hong Kong.

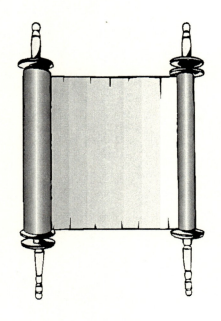

"O! Magnify the Lord with me and let us exalt

his name together.

O! taste and see that the Lord is good! Bless are

those, who trust in Him.

Psalm 34: 3 &8 KJV"

42

Back Home In Discovery Bay

After receiving my huge surprise of a *tiny bill from the accounting department of Princess Margaret Hospital*, Carrie, Gracie and I piled into a taxi for the ride back to DB. It is important to say we had to apply for a permit to use privately owned transportation several days before my discharge. Because Discovery Bay is a model community for low air pollution, the government does not allow the residents to operate personal automobiles there. We travel by walking, riding bicycles, driving a golf cart or using the public transportation the government controls. All vehicles use environmentally friendly fuel.

I missed being in DB for the thirty days while I was in Princess Margaret Hospital. I missed my friends and the things we did together. I longed for the tranquil atmosphere and the spectacular view from my apartment.

It was Christmas Eve when I returned to Discovery Bay, so many homes and some businesses and trees were decorated with beautiful lights and charming ornaments. The place was beautiful. I felt the festive sights were welcoming me back to DB. I was thrilled to be home again.

EXALTATION!!!!!!!

The facts of my traveling by ambulance forty minutes from Discovery Bay on Lan Tau Island to Princess Margaret Hospital in Kowloon in Hong Kong, having surgery the same day after an aneurysm ruptured in my brain and surviving came to mind often. Each time I recalled them, I want to go "crazy" shouting praises. I want to invite the whole world to rejoice with me.

O! Magnify the Lord with me and let us exalt his name together. O! taste and see that the Lord is good! Blessed are those, who trust in Him.
Psalm 34: 3, 8 KJV

When Gracie and I returned to my place, we rejoiced! We had much for which to give thanks. This was Gracie's first trip out of Mainland China. I wished her reasons for coming to Hong Kong were different, but I was happy and grateful to have her with me. Since we met in Dalian in 1995, we had become both "sisters" and close friends.

We arrived back in DB late afternoon. Carrie stayed with us briefly then went home. Gracie and I chatted for a while. She limited my activities and suggested I take a nap since we planned attending the Christingle Service, in celebration of Christmas, at the DB Anglican Church.

Home Again!

Returning home after thirty days absence was like visiting a strange home where I had no roots. It took me a few minutes after I walked through the apartment to realize

I was back in my own space. I had a sense of something serious happening, which had displaced me. I looked out of the large bay window in the living room at Mui Wo in the distance. I shivered a little at the thought of what could have been, but I quickly regained my composure with thoughts of gratitude for the present. I was alive! I was home again!

I felt ecstatic and extremely grateful to be well enough to attend the service on the same day I came home from the Hospital. I wanted Gracie to have another view of the Christmas celebration in addition to the glimpses she had in Dalian in 1998. Besides, Gracie had helped Carrie to make the Christingle for the celebration shortly after she arrived in Hong Kong on December 23, 2002. Seeing how the symbols she had made were used in the service would complete the experience for Gracie and introduce something new to me.

The two – hour nap refreshed me. Gracie and I got dressed in Christmas finery and went along with Carrie in a minivan to the church. When we arrived at the church, it was packed with celebrants. Although as a child, I grew up in the Anglican Church, this was my first time attending a Christingle service. It was a first for Gracie, too.

The timing was perfect. I had something to celebrate! Through God's miracles and the help of some friends, doctors, nurses, relatives and a host of other people, I had survived two ruptured brain aneurysms and brain surgery in the same year.

I became a sixty-four year old juvenile and had my youth and attitude renewed. I left the hospital after a thirty – day - extreme - makeover feeling well enough to attend a church service the same day! This is worth celebrating! HALLELUJAH!!!!

To say some people at the church were shocked to see me is a definite understatement. Some looked at me speechlessly as if they were seeing a ghost. Others, who did not expect me to survive, asked, "What are you doing here?" Some touched me just to be sure I was REAL. I chuckled and pinched myself.

Christingle

Artist Ann Margaret Pinkman

The orange represents the world. The candle is
symbolic of Jesus- Light of the world.
The red ribbon represents his blood.
The small bits of fruit and vegetables on the
skewers represent the four seasons and the good
fruits of the earth."

43

Christingle Celebration

After everyone was seated at the DB Anglican Church, the priest opened the celebration. Almost the entire service was the dramatization of the Nativity. Many children and adults took part. The scenes were replete with great music, colorful costumes and effective acting. Some children added to the joyfulness of the evening by nervously forgetting their lines or their places.

Each person got a Christingle symbol in order to participate in the candle lighting ceremony toward the end of the service. The Christingle Symbolizes the true meaning of Christmas. The significance extends beyond the Christmas celebration.

(See A WORD ABOUT CHRISTINGLE

at the end of the book)

Gracie said helping Carrie make the Christingle was an interesting experience. She had learned something to take back to her students as a cultural lesson. Each of us got a Christingle. Because of restrictions on taking fresh fruits into China from another country, Gracie had to leave hers with me. She said she studied the pattern of the Christingle and will be able to make it easily for her students.

I was overjoyed to be a participant in this celebration. I was happy I did not miss it and hoped I would live to celebrate many more. As the celebration progressed I felt enveloped by a kind of joy I wished would last forever.

One of the reasons for my joy was seeing a family, who were my neighbors when I first lived in Haven Court. Their son Adam and my grandson Jordan were playmates. I had not seen them for almost two years. Before I moved back to DB, they had moved from Haven Court to the Greens where my first miracle happened.

They were now attending church services at the DB Anglican Church. Knowing this about them filled me with much joy and affirmed divine interest in human affairs. The Christingle celebration on Christmas Eve was one indication of such interest.

HOME FOR CHRISTMAS

The morning after Gracie brought me home from the hospital, she awakened me with her soft, melodious version of, "Oh! What a beautiful morning!" from the Musical Oklahoma. It was indeed a beautiful morning!

I was grateful to be back home in Discovery Bay for Christmas after being in the hospital for thirty days.

Gracie prepared a delicious breakfast fit for two princesses. We dined in high style. The Christingle graced our table. We gave thanks for so many blessings.

We reminisced about our first Christmas together in China in 1998 when my niece Ada acted the role of Gabriel the angel, who brought good news to Virgin Mary. Ada said that was the best thing that happened to her that year. She probably still has her wings.

Whenever Gracie and I meet we sing. Singing was an important part of our English classes in Dalian China in 1995 when I was Gracie's instructor. Now, seven years later, Gracie came from Dalian, China to care for me in Hong Kong after my brain surgery. She brought gifts of compassion, a caring heart, her beautiful operatic voice and her love for singing to shower me with joy.

After breakfast on Christmas Day, Gracie and I reenacted parts of the candle lighting ceremony. We lit our Christingle and sang Christmas carols. Gracie also gave a mini concert of pieces from a Peking Opera. I felt unspeakable joy at the continuation of our Father's ordering of our steps even in the minutest detail.

This was Gracie's first trip to Hong Kong. Again, I wished the circumstances were different, and I were able to entertain her and take her sightseeing. She thought everything was fine. She had already met Carrie and her husband and several other persons, who treated her cordially. I am blessed to have great friends, who cared for my friends and me.

Gracie liked DB and enjoyed traveling to Peng Chau, a small island, only ten minutes away by boat. I bought most of my groceries, fresh fruits, vegetables, flowers and the best vegetarian pizza in Peng Chau. This was also where I did my laundry and where the closest public library and fitness center to DB are.

When I took Gracie to the laundry, she and Lola the owner became instant friends. They communicated in Mandarin. Lola graciously took time off from her work, leaving her husband in charge, and accompanied Gracie to shop on the big Hong Kong Island. Gracie almost "dropped" shopping American style. She bought many souvenirs for her family, friends and co-workers back in Dalian, China

I felt wonderful! I did not think a complete stranger would have done that for my friend. The maxim, "What goes around, comes around" made full circle for Gracie on this day. Marvelous!

Gracie thought she, too, was experiencing the "double miracles" of friendship. She had met Carrie, and Jacinth, two of my rescuers and others, who cared for her in DB before and after I was discharged from the hospital. Gracie had tasted the winning combination of eastern and western hospitality at Christmas. She wished she could have remained in Discovery Bay longer.

Well, our days were numbered. Gracie would return to Mainland China in two days, and in two weeks, I would return to America. The day after Gracie left, Peggy, another former student from Dan Dong, China came to DB to visit with me. Shortly, before Peggy left, Alaya came to help me "TIE UP LOOSE ENDS" and to pack for the trip back home. Present and former neighbors and students visited to bid us "Bon voyage!"

I am still grateful for this nurturing relay between friends and family to assist me in my transition from a lengthy hospitalization in Hong Kong to a renewed way of life in America

So Long DB!

The sweet irony is: Discovery Bay, Hong Kong has been my home since 1999 and always will be. It is impossible to erase the memories of this place that was my refuge in a storm and the site of life-saving Double miracles. DB is indeed, "The City of my Joy"

I cannot say a final good bye. Not now! Not ever!

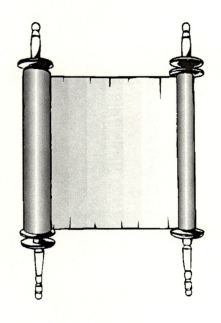

"The symptoms of brain aneurysm vary from person to person, so do the survival rates and the after effects (sequelae)"

44

Something Learned

S ome things I learned about headaches, and specifically about brain aneurysm related headaches follow:

The National Institution of Neurological Disorders and Strokes (NINDS) offers these alerts for troublesome headaches follow.

(Internet, August 2007)

In the future, I will be sure to seek medical attention immediately if any of these occur:

- An abrupt, severe headache or a sudden headache associated with a stiff neck.

- A headache associated with fever or convulsions, or accompanied by confusion or loss of consciousness.

- A headache following a blow to the head, or associated with pain in the eye or ear.

- Persistent headache in a person who was previously headache free.

- Recurring headaches in children.

I learned the following from my experience. I will be more attentive if these occur:

- I black out or faint for no apparent reason.

- My blood pressure elevates to unsafe levels

- I have a stubborn headache that is unresponsive to any type of remedy

- My eyes become sensitive to light

- I am bothered by loud sounds

- I describe my headache as 20 on a scale of one to ten – the worst headache of my life.

- My headache is accompanied by nausea and or vomiting.

- I am hearing voices, or I am hallucinating.

- I experience bouts of temporary amnesia.

- I WILL NEVER IGNORE A HEADACHE

- I will call the emergency medical services, or I will ask someone to call if any of the above conditions exists.

- I will have personal and medical history, list of medications, doctors and emergency contacts available at all times.

- I will have an overnight case packed with these and other appropriate items for hospital admission.

Motivations

Surviving two ruptured brain aneurysms has motivated me to use the energies of my restored life to learn more facts about the human body and health, which may help others and me. Today, I am more educated about headaches, their causes and treatment.

I tell my experience as a first step in encouraging anyone, who suffers from persistent aches in head and neck or strange burnings and creepy-crawly sensations in the head, to seek medical help. It is imperative, if there is a family history of cerebral hemorrhage, brain tumors or brain aneurysms, to seek medical help and apply preventive measures.

*The symptoms of brain aneurysm vary from person to person, so do the survival rates and the after effects (**sequelae**).* My mother Mabelle Maud Sloly, my sister Irene Advenia Stewart and I were among the blessed to survive physically intact although we suffered some cognitive defects and memory loss.

My sister and I are plagued by frequent headaches, which we believe will vanish when we learn more about managing causative agents. These may include foods, beverages chemicals and **stressful environments.**

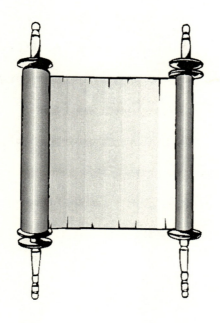

I will always praise the Lord.

With all my heart I will praise the Lord.

Let all who are helpless, listen and be glad.

Honor the Lord with me!

Celebrate His great name.

I asked the Lord for help

and he saved me from all my fears.

Keep your eyes on the Lord!

You will shine as the sun and

never blush with shame.

I was a nobody, but I prayed

And the Lord saved me from all my troubles.

If you honor the Lord,

His angels will protect you.

Discover for yourself that the Lord is kind.

Come to Him for protection and you will be glad.

Psalm 34:1-8 (CEV)

45

Epilogue

My story of surviving two ruptured brain aneurysms, a major medical catastrophe, could be duplicated many times over by people, who have experienced nothing less than miracles in their medical histories. While it is difficult to tell with clarity the miraculous, it is easy to show the gratitude of an appreciative heart.

My grateful heart feels compelled to tell her story and in doing so, inspire many people, who want to tell theirs. This book is the product of my grateful heart. I wrote it as an expression of gratitude for supernatural and human interventions, which saved me from certain death in Discovery Bay, Hong Kong.

Writing this book was easy and difficult.

It is easy for me to express my gratitude. I learned how difficult it is to undertake a major writing project after suffering a life threatening insult to my brain.

When I wrote my dissertation in 1990, it took seven months. I was in good health and was able to stay up sleeplessly for several consecutive days and nights to research endlessly, think deeply and write furiously. I had to behave differently for this assignment.

This is by far the most challenging writing project I have undertaken. It took me more than two years to write a story, which is already over five years old. Several times, I had to postpone writing to cope with recurring headaches, labile blood pressure and frequent hospitalizations. I also took time off to care for family members in Montclair New Jersey.

Completing this testimony of my Creator's goodness is a triumph over the potential devastating effects of ruptured brain aneurysms and brain surgery. It was a monumental task to recall some memories I thought I had lost forever. It was impossible to write without reliving the experiences.

Some parts of the story were disturbing in ways that shocked, shamed, bewildered and bothered me. I was tearful when I recalled the people who died while I lived. I agonized for the infants, who had craniotomy and for their devoted parents.

I present only what I could recall. The chronology may be out of sequence, but the events are accurate. I only wish my presentation were free of the pestering typos, reversals, omissions, incorrect word choice and even some spelling errors. Although several people read and made corrections to the manuscript, it is still conceivable to have missed some evasive errors.

As you read, I implore you to look beyond these to the content; however, if you find items, which affect the flow of the story, please tell me of them in an email to *marlenovec@ yahoo.com* or drnovec@bellsouth.net. I will be most grateful.

You may also ask questions or make comments at these email addresses. You may also call me at 954-724-8382.

I trust my story will encourage you to continue being attentive to your health and to cherish your life as your creator's precious gift to you. May you live the rest of your days exquisitely in maximum health as **He completes the good things He began in you.**

Please accept my deep gratitude and appreciation for your company on my incredible journey from my child-hood in Jamaica through the "valley of the of the shadow of death" in Discovery Bay, Hong Kong to the plateau of restored health and joyful living in the world.

Marlegrecy N'Ovec, Ed.D.

A.

A WORD ABOUT:

ACKEE

Ackeee: A variation is Akee. The origin is unknown, but it has been in the English language since 1794. Akee is the fleshy fruit of an African tree of the soapberry family grown in the Caribbean and Florida area and Hawaii. It is edible when ripe, but has a toxic raphe attaching the aril to the seed and toxic aril when immature or overripe.

Free Internet Source

B.

A WORD ABOUT

CHRISTINGLE

Artist Ann Margaret Pinkman, Montclair,

New Jersey

The Christingle

The Christingle is a symbol, which originated in Germany. It was first used in the Moravian Church in a children's Christmas service on Christmas Eve 1747.

Then it was just a lighted candle tied with a red ribbon in memory of the "Saviour's coming", which the bishop hoped would keep burning in each heart "to His joy and our happiness".

The Christingle symbol has expanded to include:

- *An orange –* **representing the world**

- *A red ribbon tied around the orange to represent Jesus' blood*

- *Four cocktail sticks to represent spring, summer, winter and fall*

- *Sweets and fruits representing the abundance of God's gifts from the earth. These are skewered onto the cocktail sticks and pushed into the orange around the candle.*

- *A lighted candle signifying Christ as the "Light of the world" This is pushed in the center of the orange.*

Free Internet Source

C.

A WORD ABOUT:

Hebrew Names for God and Their Simply Meanings

Taken from The Ryrie Study Bible King James Version

Page 1875

There are many others. Jehovah prefaces these:

Jehovah Jireh – The Lord provides, Genesis 22:14;

Jehovah Nissi – The Lord is my Banner, Exodus 17:1

Jehovah Shalom – The lord is Peace, Judges 6:24

Jehovah Sabbaoth – The Lord of Host, I Samuel 1:3

Jehovah Raah – The lord is my Shepherd, Psalm 23:1

Jehovah Shammah – The Lord is There, Ezekiel 48:3

Jehovah Tsidkenu – The Lord our Righteousness, Jeremiah 23:6; Jehovah Maccaddeshcem – The Lord our Sanctifier, Exodus 31:13; Jehovah Elohim – The Lord God of Israel, Judges 5:3; Isaiah 17:6

D.

A WORD ABOUT:

Marlegrecy N'Ovec, Ed.D.

Double Miracles in Discovery Bay, Hong Kong

Volume II

FOR YOUR JOURNEY

Knitted by Guo Yan Ling

Artist Vidal R. Linton

<u>**For Your Journey:**</u> is the continuation of my story of surviving ruptured brain aneurysms. My son Vidal Linton, artist of the boots pictured above, will be the chief illustrator.

This volume is already being written and will be published soon.

Printed in the United States
131508LV00001BA/2/P

9 781606 472491